Danger in the Past

33 1/3 Global

33 1/3 Global, a series related to but independent from **33 1/3**, takes the format of the original series of short, music-based books and brings the focus to music throughout the world. With initial volumes focusing on Japanese and Brazilian music, the series will also include volumes on the popular music of Australia/Oceania, Europe, Africa, the Middle East, and more.

33 1/3 Japan

Series Editor: Noriko Manabe

Spanning a range of artists and genres – from the 1970s rock of Happy End to technopop band Yellow Magic Orchestra, the Shibuya-kei of Cornelius, classic anime series *Cowboy Bebop*, J-Pop/EDM hybrid Perfume, and vocaloid star Hatsune Miku – **33 1/3 Japan** is a series devoted to in-depth examination of Japanese popular music of the twentieth and twenty-first centuries.

Published Titles:
Supercell's *Supercell* by Keisuke Yamada
AKB48 by Patrick W. Galbraith and Jason G. Karlin
Yoko Kanno's *Cowboy Bebop Soundtrack* by Rose Bridges
Perfume's *Game* by Patrick St. Michel
Cornelius's *Fantasma* by Martin Roberts
Joe Hisaishi's *My Neighbor Totoro: Soundtrack* by Kunio Hara
Shonen Knife's *Happy Hour* by Brooke McCorkle
Nenes' *Koza Dabasa* by Henry Johnson
Yuming's *The 14th Moon* by Lasse Lehtonen
Toshiko Akiyoshi-Lew Tabackin Big Band's *Kogun* by E. Taylor Atkins
S.O.B.'s *Don't Be Swindle* by Mahon Murphy and Ran Zwigenberg

Forthcoming Titles:
Kohaku Utagassen: The Red and White Song Contest by Shelley Brunt
Yellow Magic Orchestra's *Yellow Magic Orchestra* by Toshiyuki Ohwada

33 1/3 Brazil

Series Editor: Jason Stanyek

Covering the genres of samba, tropicália, rock, hip hop, forró, bossa nova, heavy metal and funk, among others, **33 1/3 Brazil** is a series devoted to in-depth examination of the most important Brazilian albums of the twentieth and twenty-first centuries.

Published Titles:

Caetano Veloso's *A Foreign Sound* by Barbara Browning

Tim Maia's *Tim Maia Racional Vols. 1 &2* by Allen Thayer

João Gilberto and Stan Getz's *Getz/Gilberto* by Brian McCann

Gilberto Gil's *Refazenda* by Marc A. Hertzman

Dona Ivone Lara's *Sorriso Negro* by Mila Burns

Milton Nascimento and Lô Borges's *The Corner Club* by Jonathon Grasse

Racionais MCs' *Sobrevivendo no Inferno* by Derek Pardue

Naná Vasconcelos's *Saudades* by Daniel B. Sharp

Chico Buarque's First *Chico Buarque* by Charles A. Perrone

Forthcoming titles:

Jorge Ben Jor's *África Brasil* by Frederick J. Moehn

33 1/3 Europe

Series Editor: Fabian Holt

Spanning a range of artists and genres, **33 1/3 Europe** offers engaging accounts of popular and culturally significant albums of Continental Europe and the North Atlantic from the twentieth and twenty-first centuries.

Published Titles:

Darkthrone's *A Blaze in the Northern Sky* by Ross Hagen

Ivo Papazov's *Balkanology* by Carol Silverman

Heiner Müller and Heiner Goebbels's *Wolokolamsker Chaussee* by Philip V. Bohlman

Modeselektor's *Happy Birthday!* by Sean Nye
Mercyful Fate's *Don't Break the Oath* by Henrik Marstal
Bea Playa's *I'll Be Your Plaything* by Anna Szemere and András Rónai
Various Artists' *DJs do Guetto* by Richard Elliott
Czesław Niemen's *Niemen Enigmatic* by Ewa Mazierska and Mariusz Gradowski
Massada's *Astaganaga* by Lutgard Mutsaers
Los Rodriguez's *Sin Documentos* by Fernán del Val and Héctor Fouce
Édith Piaf's *Récital 1961* by David Looseley
Nuovo Canzoniere Italiano's *Bella Ciao* by Jacopo Tomatis
Iannis Xenakis's *Persepolis* by Aram Yardumian
Vopli Vidopliassova's *Tantsi* by Maria Sonevytsky
Amália Rodrigues's *Amália at the Olympia* by Lila Ellen Gray
Ardit Gjebrea's *Projekt Jon* by Nicholas Tochka
Aqua's *Aquarium* by C.C. McKee
J. M. K. E.'s *To the Cold Land* by Brigitta Davidjants
Taco Hemingway's *Jarmark* by Kamila Rymajdo
Einstürzende Neubauten's *Kollaps* by Melle Jan Kromhout and Jan Nieuwenhuis

Forthcoming Titles:
Silly's *Februar* by Michael Rauhut
CCCP's *Fedeli Alla Linea's 1964–1985 Affinità-Divergenze Fra Il Compagno Togliatti E Noi Del Conseguimento Della Maggiore Età* by Giacomo Bottà
Sigur Rós' *Ágætis Byrjun* by Tore Størvold

33 1/3 Oceania

Series Editors: Jon Stratton (senior editor) and Jon Dale (specializing in books on albums from Aotearoa/New Zealand)

Spanning a range of artists and genres from Australian Indigenous artists to Maori and Pasifika artists, from Aotearoa/New Zealand noise music to Australian rock, and including music from Papua and other

Pacific islands, **33 1/3 Oceania** offers exciting accounts of albums that illustrate the wide range of music made in the Oceania region.

Published Titles:
John Farnham's *Whispering Jack* by Graeme Turner
The Church's *Starfish* by Chris Gibson
Regurgitator's *Unit* by Lachlan Goold and Lauren Istvandity
Kylie Minogue's *Kylie* by Adrian Renzo and Liz Giuffre
Alastair Riddell's *Space Waltz* by Ian Chapman
Hunters & Collectors's *Human Frailty* by Jon Stratton
The Front Lawn's *Songs from the Front Lawn* by Matthew Bannister
Bic Runga's *Drive* by Henry Johnson
The Dead C's *Clyma est mort* by Darren Jorgensen
Ed Kuepper's *Honey Steel's Gold* by John Encarnacao
Chain's *Toward the Blues* by Peter Beilharz
Hilltop Hoods' *The Calling* by Dianne Rodger
Screamfeeder's *Kitten Licks* by Ben Green and Ian Rogers
The Clean's *Boodle Boodle Boodle* by Geoff Stahl
The Avalanches' *Since I Left You* by Charles Fairchild
John Sangster's *Lord of the Rings Vols. 1–3* by Bruce Johnson
Soundtrack from *Saturday Night Fever* by Clinton Walker
Eyeliner's *BUY NOW* by Michael Brown
TISM's *Machiavelli and the Four Seasons* by Tyler Jenke
Crowded House's *Together Alone* by Barnaby Smith
silverchair's *Frogstomp* by Jay Daniel Thompson
Various Artists' *A Truckload of Sky: The Lost Songs of David McComb* by Glenn D'Cruz
Robert Forster's *Danger in the Past* by Patrick Chapman

Forthcoming Titles:
The Triffids' *Born Sandy Devotional* by Christina Ballico
5MMM's *Compilation Album of Adelaide Bands 1980* by Collette Snowden

INXS' *Kick* by Lauren Moxey
Sunnyboys' *Sunnyboys* by Stephen Bruel
The La De Das' *The Happy Prince* by John Tebbutt
Gary Shearston's *Dingo* by Peter Mills
Kate Ceberano's *Brave* by Panizza Allmark
Dinah Lee's *Introducing Dinah Lee* by Kimberly Cannady
The Waifs' *Up All Night* by Rebecca Bennison
The Three Out's *Move* by James Gaunt
Split Enz' *Mental Notes* by Michael Lamb
Tame Impala's *Currents* by Alister Newstead
Douglas Lilburn's *Complete Electro-Acoustic Works* by Bruce Russell
Savage Garden's *Affirmation* by Pat O'Grady
Dick Diver's *Calendar Days* by Mitch L. Ryan

33 1/3 South Asia

Series Editor: Natalie Sarrazin

From the films of Bollywood and Lollywood, to home-grown *bhangra* hip hop, Hindu devotional pop and Sufi rock, Sri Lankan rap, Indo jazz and disco, new-wave electronica and diasporic Asian Underground scene, **33 1/3 South Asia** takes readers on a sonically diverse journey through the most significant soundtracks and albums from the twentieth and twenty-first centuries.

Published:

Dil Chahta Hai Soundtrack by Jayson Beaster-Jones
Lata Mangeshkar's *My Favourites, Volume 2* by Anirudha Bhattacharjee
 and Chandrashekhar Rao
Coke Studio (Season 14) by Rakae Rehman Jamil and Khadija Muzaffar

33 1/3 Africa

Series Editor: Michael Veal

33 1/3 Africa is a series of books on canonical, album-length works of African music including traditional music, experimental music, and, with particular emphasis, popular music. Academic and journalistic writing results in sophisticated, nuanced and accessible narratives on African music.

Published:
Fela Anikulapo-Kuti's *Sorrow Tears and Blood* by Stephanie Shonekan

Forthcoming Titles:
Cesária Évora's *Miss Perfumado* by Jacqueline Georgis
Paul Simon's *Graceland* by Kalvin Schmidt-Rimpler Dinh
Nico, Rochereau, Roger & L'African Fiesta – *Volume 1 (1962–1963)* by Frank Gunderson

Danger in the Past

Patrick Chapman

Series Editors: Jon Stratton, UniSA Creative, University of South Australia, and Jon Dale, University of Melbourne, Australia

BLOOMSBURY ACADEMIC
NEW YORK • LONDON • OXFORD • NEW DELHI • SYDNEY

BLOOMSBURY ACADEMIC

Bloomsbury Publishing Inc, 1385 Broadway, New York, NY 10018, USA
Bloomsbury Publishing Plc, 50 Bedford Square, London, WC1B 3DP, UK
Bloomsbury Publishing Ireland, 29 Earlsfort Terrace, Dublin 2, D02 AY28, Ireland

BLOOMSBURY, BLOOMSBURY ACADEMIC and the Diana logo are trademarks of
Bloomsbury Publishing Plc

First published in the United States of America 2025

Copyright © Patrick Chapman, 2025

For legal purposes the Acknowledgments on p. xv constitute an extension of this copyright page.

All rights reserved. No part of this publication may be: i) reproduced or transmitted in any form, electronic or mechanical, including photocopying, recording or by means of any information storage or retrieval system without prior permission in writing from the publishers; or ii) used or reproduced in any way for the training, development or operation of artificial intelligence (AI) technologies, including generative AI technologies. The rights holders expressly reserve this publication from the text and data mining exception as per Article 4(3) of the Digital Single Market Directive (EU) 2019/790.

Bloomsbury Publishing Inc does not have any control over, or responsibility for, any third-party websites referred to or in this book. All internet addresses given in this book were correct at the time of going to press. The author and publisher regret any inconvenience caused if addresses have changed or sites have ceased to exist, but can accept no responsibility for any such changes.

Library of Congress Cataloging-in-Publication Data

Names: Chapman, Patrick, 1968- author.
Title: Danger in the past / Patrick Chapman.
Other titles: Robert Forster's Danger in the past
Description: [1.] | New York : Bloomsbury Academic, 2025. | Series: 33 1/3 Oceania | Includes bibliographical references and index. | Summary: "Dublin, Ireland. That World Cup summer of 1990. A 21-year-old poet is entranced by The Go-Betweens: 1978-1990. As the city outside goes football crazy, the poet discovers his new favorite band and learns that he'll never see them live; they have recently split up. That same day, Robert Forster is celebrating his 33rd birthday and recording his solo album Danger in the Past at Hansa Studios, Berlin, with members of the Bad Seeds. This book introduces an enduring album to new listeners while offering the ultimate companion to fans who regard Danger in the Past as a true 'rock'n'roll friend.'"– Provided by publisher.
Identifiers: LCCN 2025010956 | ISBN 9798765128084 (hardback) | ISBN 9798765128077 (paperback) | ISBN 9798765128091 (epub) | ISBN 9798765128107 (pdf)
Subjects: LCSH: Forster, Robert (Vocalist). Danger in the past. | Rock music--Australia--1981-1990--History and criticism.
Classification: LCC ML420.F7542 C53 2025 | DDC 782.42166092--dc23/eng/20250318
LC record available at https://lccn.loc.gov/2025010956

ISBN: HB: 979-8-7651-2808-4
PB: 979-8-7651-2807-7
ePDF: 979-8-7651-2810-7
eBook: 979-8-7651-2809-1

Series: 33 1/3 Oceania

Typeset by Deanta Global Publishing Services, Chennai, India
Printed and bound in the United States of America

For product safety related questions contact productsafety@bloomsbury.com.

To find out more about our authors and books visit www.bloomsbury.com and sign up for our newsletters.

To Sara

Contents

Acknowledgements xv
Album Credits xvi
Preface xviii

The Past

1 *The Go-Betweens 1978–1990* 3

2 The sound of young Brisbane 11

3 Love is a sign 27

4 Intermission 39

Another Country

5 A ballroom in Berlin 45

6 Hansa memories 51

7 The songs 63

Doing Things Differently

8 The anchor 85

9 *Freakchild* **variations** 91

10 Mythologies 95

11 Needle drops 105

12 Portraits of the artist 111

13 A classic? 117

Discography 123
Notes 128
Bibliography 140
Index 141

Acknowledgements

Thanks to Robert Forster for our meeting in London to discuss *Danger in the Past* and to his managers Bob Johnson and Bernard Galbally. Thanks also to Mick Harvey and Thomas Wydler for kindly answering my interview questions by email; to Pete Paphides for our phone conversation about the Needle Mythology reissue and his memories of the Go-Betweens and Robert; to Seán A. McDermott for his insights into how the Go-Betweens, as well as Robert Forster solo, inspired a younger musical scene in Dublin; to Éamonn Davis for introducing me to the blue double-album in 1990; to Rachel Moore and her colleagues at Bloomsbury Academic for commissioning the book; and to my editor Jon Stratton at 33 1/3 Oceania for his wisdom and guidance from start to finish. All of the above made the present volume possible. Special thanks to Sara Mullen, my wife, whose love and support sustained me in so many ways during the writing of this book.

Lyrics reproduced by kind permission of Domino Songs Ltd.

Album Credits

Danger in the Past

Side One

Baby Stones	4:07
The River People	3:25
Leave Here Satisfied	4:59
Heart Out to Tender	4:14
Is This What You Call Change	2:38

Side Two

Dear Black Dream	6:04
Danger in the Past	4:50
I've Been Looking for Somebody	4:20
Justice	3:45

Personnel

Robert Forster: guitar, vocals

Mick Harvey: Hammond organ, bass, percussion, piano, guitar and vocals

Thomas Wydler: drums

with

Hugo Race: lead and rhythm guitar on 'Leave Here Satisfied', 'Heart Out to Tender', 'Dear Black Dream' and 'Danger in the Past'

Karin Bäumler: vocals on 'Danger in the Past'

Produced by Mick Harvey

Recorded and mixed by Victor Van Vugt at Hansa Tonstudios and at Preußen Tonstudios, Berlin, West Germany from 20 June to 4 July 1990

Originally released by Beggars Banquet in 1990

Reissued by Needle Mythology under licence from Beggars Banquet in 2020

Remastered by Sean Magee at Abbey Road Studios, London

Preface

There's an intimate feeling in the Gutter Bookshop as Robert Forster reads from *Grant & I*, his elegant new memoir, and discusses it with Roisín Dwyer of *Hot Press*. This Friday in Dublin is the fourth date of his book tour, 8 September 2017, and around thirty people, who may or may not look like Dostoevsky,[1] sit rapt a few feet away from their musical hero. Robert recalls Grant McLennan, his late friend and bandmate, the subject of his book. He sings and strums a few songs on his guitar. Outside on Cow's Lane, a veil of grey drizzle has fallen, but tonight, in this beautiful bookshop, inclement weather matters not a bit.

Standing before Robert in the signing queue, I'm almost used to the sensation, having met him many times like this since the first, when he played Dublin's Mean Fiddler in 1996 on the *Warm Nights* tour. On that occasion, I only had my ticket for him to autograph. When I said I should have brought *Danger in the Past*, he agreed, 'Yeah, you should've'.

I've brought it tonight. He signs my copy of his memoir, then I present my CD booklet of his debut album.

'It's a classic', he says.

'A classic', he writes on the booklet as if to confirm it.

As we meet now, it's been twelve years since the Go-Betweens enjoyed the best reviews of their career for *Oceans Apart*. It's been eleven since Grant McLennan died of a heart attack on the day of his house-warming party, just as the band had begun to get its due. I am reminded of Jean Rhys's response to the long-delayed appreciation she received in old age, on the publication of *Wide Sargasso Sea*: 'It has come too late.'[2]

And still, for Robert Forster, it has come.

In the decades since his old band ended for the first time, his reputation has grown and deepened. These days, his songs tend to need a lot of time to marinate, inviting patience in the audience as well as in himself, but when they arrive, they are greeted like old friends.

To paraphrase the Oscar Wilde epigram[3] from which this bookshop gets its name – tonight we are all in the Gutter, and some of us are looking at a star.

The Past

1 *The Go-Betweens 1978–1990*

I first heard Robert Forster's voice one Saturday afternoon in a flat attached to the Quaker meeting house on Eustace Street, Dublin. Some pals who were staying there had invited me up to pass the time before we went to see the Ireland vs. Italy game at the Underground bar around the corner on Dame Street.

Our host, the songwriter and guitarist Éamonn Davis, took out a new double album and put the first disc on. Its cover was eye-catching: a spray of sunlit hornbeam leaves against a shimmering blue sky. The record's title, *The Go-Betweens 1978–1990*, hung in a lavender oval above the trees.

With the opening track, I fell in love. 'Karen'. I'd never heard anything like this obsessive hymn to a librarian. Then again, I'd not heard much until coming to the city a few years before, to attend college. I was always hungry for new sounds, and this album proved to be a feast that would nourish me for years.

It was natural that Éamonn should admire the Go-Betweens and its songwriters, Robert Forster and Grant McLennan. Inspired also by Edwyn Collins and Postcard[1] – The Sound of Young Scotland – his band Hey, Paulette! often played the Underground, then a key venue for independent music in Dublin. Hey, Paulette! recorded a John Peel session and released jangle-pop singles on Ireland's hippest label, Mickey Rourke's Fridge.

Just as Australian groups such as the Go-Betweens, the Birthday Party and the Triffids went to the UK to try and make it big, so did many Irish artists. Cork band Microdisney signed to Rough Trade in 1983, where they were labelmates with the Go-Betweens and released their classic album *The Clock Comes Down the Stairs*. After moving to Virgin Records, they put out two more LPs and had minor hits in both Ireland and the UK before breaking up.[2] Dublin band the Stars of Heaven released two albums on Rough Trade, *Sacred Heart Hotel* (1986) and *Speak Slowly* (1988), before calling it a day. Something Happens and the Hothouse Flowers were others who signed international deals in the days before Irish indie music became a commercial prospect with the likes of the Cranberries crossing over into the mainstream.

For those who stayed at home, there were the local labels. Mickey Rourke's Fridge was founded by singer-songwriter Seán A. McDermott as a true indie. *Hot Press*, Ireland's music paper, often used the word 'eclectic' when discussing artists who were different, and the bands on Mickey Rourke's Fridge were certainly that. In a town beset by heroin, mass unemployment and economic depression, Seán had convened a stable of optimists making their own way in the world, playing in each other's pop groups[3] and putting out excellent 7" and 12" records. To showcase the abundance of talent that flowed through it, MRF also released compilations on cassette, including *Dostoevsky Lose its Flavour on the Bedpost Overnight*.[4] Seán McDermott's own group, the Wayfaring Strangers, made what would now be called alt-country music, his vocal style coming across like Lou Reed singing Gram Parsons. No wonder that Forster and McLennan, rather than, say, U2, were the real heroes to these artists for whom the big time might never arrive, but music was ever present.

Seán McDermott and I discussed how in some respects the indie scene in early 1990s Dublin resembled that of Brisbane when the Go-Betweens were starting.[5]

PC: It seems to me that in both Brisbane and Dublin, punk's DIY ethos inspired bands that didn't always necessarily produce punk music.

SMcD: There were similar roots to those two scenes, even before the Go-Betweens, like Big Star, Gram Parsons and obviously the Velvet Underground. Some of the people Robert has referred to as his brothers David and Tom – David Byrne and Tom Verlaine – were also influences on us. We were coming from the same place, only 10,000 miles away. Oceans apart, if you will. The Go-Betweens were a very big influence on Hey Paulette!, more so than Big Star or the Velvets. The chiming guitars, that striped sunlight sound, is something we all went back to every now and then, along with country music sometimes. You bring that [striped sunlight] into country, and it sounds great.

PC: As a young person in music back then, what did the Go-Betweens mean to you?

SMcD: I bought their record, the single, because it was on Postcard. I thought, this is a bit odd. Then I heard the second album and thought, this is amazing. It was similar to what they were doing on the single, but they seemed to have a totally new approach to the dynamics of the three instruments: the bass, the drums and the guitar. It was amazing and inspiring and although we'd never tried to sound like them it happened by accident because we were drawing from the same well.

PC: Did that compilation seem like the end or the beginning of something?

SMcD: It did seem like a lifetime achievement award, as if this was the end of something and that something else would happen, which obviously it did. Apart from the first record [on the double set] and its not-hits, that second disc ends with 'You Won't Find It Again', a Grant song. I love that song, and I even learned how to play it.

PC: When *Danger in the Past* was released, did it feel different? Obviously, the dynamic was going to be different from that of the Go-Betweens, but was there anything else?

SMcD: I was pleasantly surprised to see that Mick Harvey was on it. When the Go-Betweens got the bass player [Robert Vickers] in, and Grant switched to guitar, that was a big change as well. And you might think that Robert Forster playing with a band would sound the same, but it didn't at all. It was something different, a detour.

PC: There was something in the air then, as Robert started to go for country and Americana sounds.

SMcD: Yes, and Grant started doing that on his solo albums as well. Before then, they'd done a pastiche thing, 'Don't Call Me Gone', but this was genuine; even less of a pastiche than the Rolling Stones, say. It was just something that both of them brought to the fore at the same time, coincidentally.

PC: Did *Danger in the Past* seem like a literary record?

SMcD: From the cover in, yes. I love that picture, and the title track is more of a recitation than a song. It could be like a short story. It reminded me of a Jay McInerney story where the protagonist is doing rehab. He's one of the characters in the Calloway novels[6] and he comes to the fore in this short story, and you get him calling from a country phone; that's another coincidence. Maybe not the full record is literary, but that title track certainly sounds like it could have been typed out and read very well.

PC: Robert Forster thinks the song is a miracle, and he doesn't quite know where it came from. He appears to be in awe of it.

SMcD: Even though it was recognizably the same person, it was also recognizably a different approach he was taking, and not just because of Mick Harvey's influence. It may have been his new approach that led him to Harvey.

PC: He wasn't doing grunge or the Pixies sound. As he has said, for this record, his influences were more in the singer-songwriter territory.

SMcD: He was timeless. Anyone who's a big Dylan fan, like he was, is going to end up playing country eventually. Funny to think my favourite songs from that record and Grant's had 'stones' in the title.[7]

PC: When Éamonn Davis played *The Go-Betweens 1978–1990* to me, it was the perfect introduction to the band.

SMcD: That's a good place to start, listening to that first, then going back to the earlier Go-Betweens albums. It's like reading *Ulysses* then going on to read *Dubliners* or maybe *Portrait of the Artist*. But *Danger in the Past* is nothing like *Finnegans Wake*, thank God.

Clinton Walker, author of *Stranded*,[8] recalls how his review of *1978–1990* upset Grant with its suggestion that the band had played the same solo for ten years. Lindy Morrison, the Go-Betweens' uniquely talented drummer, and Amanda Brown, who played violin and more, took elements of the review as a sexist dismissal of their contributions. However, Walker was satirizing a common putdown rather than restating it, a subtlety perhaps lost in print. His assessment of the compilation itself is right on the money:

> This album illuminates the Go-Betweens' great achievements, their glorious folly and their almost transcendent artifice.[9] (Walker, pp. 255)

Listening to the first LP of better-known songs and the second disc of B-sides and rare tracks, I admired the band's sensibility. 'The Clarke Sisters' mentions period blood, 'the flood of love', with a directness that would surely have barred it from the mainstream radio playlists of the day.[10] 'Draining the Pool for You', an anthem for the exploited, has a refreshing dash of snark in the service of what we would now call the ninety-nine per cent. 'Cattle and Cane' remains sublime, Grant's greatest song,[11] yet 'The Wrong Road' struck me first with the line: 'When the rain hit the roof with the sound of a finished kiss.' In those days at least, many Go-Betweens fans enjoyed them for their lyrics as much as for their music.

With his unmistakable voice in terms of both singing and writing, Robert's songs came to mean more to me over time than did Grant's. 'Spring Rain' slipped into my mind and danced in exactly the same way that it didn't move my feet. 'Love Is a Sign', with its impossible opening couplet, was itself a sign towards the future: 'I'm ten feet underwater, standing in a sunken canoe.'

The Go-Betweens 1978–1990, compiled by Robert and Grant while on the *16 Lovers Lane* tour, was a celebration of such dreamers as themselves, often misunderstood but vindicated in the end. It would also prove to be the original band's valedictory statement.

I didn't know it, but that afternoon before a World Cup football game – 30 June 1990 – was the day after Robert Forster's thirty-third birthday. Nor did I know that he was in West Berlin, recording his debut solo album at Hansa.

When *Danger in the Past* came out on 3 September, I had just turned twenty-two and was completing my first collection of poetry. Robert's lyrical approach confirmed something for me, that as a writer I had to be true to my own voice, or at least to my own artifice. I had found this before in the lyrics of David Byrne on his album, *Music for the Knee Plays*.[12] I had seen it in my early poetic influences: Sylvia Plath, Anne Sexton, Elizabeth Bishop and Rainer Maria Rilke.[13] At the same time, Robert was also steeped in some of those poets, notably Sexton, as well as Adrienne Rich and Patti Smith.

If, according to L. P. Hartley's novel *The Go-Between*,[14] the past is another country where they do things differently,[15] it is also, as William Faulkner put it, never dead and is not even past.[16] Sometimes that's a good thing. First on the Beggars Banquet cassette, then on CD for my Discman, and finally on the Needle Mythology vinyl release, *Danger in the Past* has been my rock'n'roll friend for well over 33 1/3 years.

2 The sound of young Brisbane

I did not grow up in a police state, although the Ireland of my youth was ultra-conservative in a familiar postcolonial way: once we had gained partial independence from Britain, we immediately handed ourselves over to the Catholic hierarchy. In our republic, divorce was not allowed; condoms, abortion and male homosexual acts[1] were all illegal; many books and films were banned, and several authors were driven into exile, albeit unofficially.[2] The church, with its Magdalene laundries, clerical abuse and hidden corruption, wielded pernicious control. Certain politicians lived large while lecturing ordinary people to tighten their belts.[3] Hypocrisy was the lubricant that helped the machinery of our society run without creaking so loudly it would wake us up. We didn't quite know how to be free, and although we may now look back on those times from the perspective of having liberalized somewhat, our legacy of deference, our tendency to conform is not entirely gone.

Unlike me, Robert Forster did grow up in a police state. The Bjelke-Petersen government in Queensland held power for almost two decades through the manipulation of the electoral process, the suppression of dissent and the collusion of the police, whose brutality during that period became notorious.[4]

It would be improper to conclude that this state of political malaise was exactly the same as in Ireland or in other places where a departing empire has left an emotionally injured population behind it. Yet I see certain similarities. People born into a postcolonial society are born into distortion. If they don't understand this, let alone recognize it, they will usually find ways to mask the damage they have inherited as well as that which they may inflict. This goes for artists as well as alcoholics; for ordinary citizens as well as those on whom they look down. If every mirror is cracked, denial is one of the stronger colours refracted.

In the Brisbane of 'hillbilly dictator' Joh Bjelke-Petersen, denial was a way of life. When in 1971 his government declared a month-long state of emergency in response to anti-apartheid protests against the Springbok tour, Australia still had remnants of racist legislation on its books. That legislation would finally be repealed by the socially progressive federal government of Gough Whitlam, which was itself to be removed by the Governor General John Kerr during the constitutional crisis of 1975. Whitlam, unlike others, did not believe that the CIA was involved in his dismissal, although his reformist agenda was unpopular in those bastions of democracy, Whitehall and the White House. He was onto Bjelke-Petersen and called him a 'Bible-bashing bastard'.[5]

As the decade wore on, the Queensland regime became ever more repressive while remaining popular with the rural electorate. Punk music, seen as intensely political, was used as an excuse to control the young and the inconvenient. With its compliant police, the government cracked down on social gatherings of which it didn't approve, leaching the warmth out of everyday life and setting Brisbane on a joyless path into the cultural desert. Andrew Stafford, in his survey of Brisbane music, *Pig City*,[6] describes the situation thus:

> Bjelke-Petersen's rule of Queensland between 1968 and 1987 was nothing if not iron-fisted. Public displays of dissent were often brutally suppressed: the rule of law was routinely bent to the will of those charged with its enforcement: minorities were treated as simply another obstacle on the path to development. To top it all off, the electoral system was hopelessly rigged in favour of the incumbents. (Stafford, pp. 2)

Stafford rejects easy answers, however, believing that punk happened more as a reaction to a stultifying culture frozen in time than to the regime:

> it makes little sense to give a politician too much credit for the creation of a music scene. Major cultural movements result from an intersection of local, national and international factors. The Saints were not so much a reaction to living in a police state as they were a response to the music of not just the Stooges and the MC5, but the Easybeats and the Missing Links.[7] (Stafford, pp. 2)

Brisbane's punk counterculture centred on the fiercely anti-Joh radio station 4ZZZ (usually pronounced Triple Zed).[8] Based in the University of Queensland until 1978, 4ZZZ was founded by activists in 1975, a week after the dismissal of Gough Whitlam. The first song it played was 'Won't Get Fooled Again' by the Who. On 19 November 1979, the station broadcast a concert by the Go-Betweens.

In 2001, 4ZZZ released a compilation album, *Behind the Banana Curtain*, documenting the local music scene it had championed during its first twenty-five years. Appropriately, the album opens with the Saints' '(I'm) Stranded'. The group released the song in September 1976, a month before the Damned put out 'New Rose' in the UK. This makes '(I'm) Stranded' the first punk single released outside the United States. In Australia, it influenced much of what would follow.

The second song on *Behind the Banana Curtain* is 'Karen' by the Go-Betweens. Intentional or not, the juxtaposition with '(I'm) Stranded' neatly illustrates the diversity of Brisbane punk and post-punk.

A pivotal track is 'Pig City', written by Tony Kniepp and recorded over two weeks by the Parameters in December 1983, using 4ZZZ's facilities. The song, an anti-police rallying cry, oinking vocals and all, explicitly criticizes the regime and became an Australian punk standard. It went on to give its name to Andrew Stafford's book, and to a Queensland Music Festival event in 2007. An earlier song, 'Task Force' by Razar, released in 1978 with the instruction on the sleeve: ONLY TO BE PLAYED LOUD, is straight-ahead political punk reminiscent of Northern Ireland's Stiff Little Fingers. Ben Ely of Regurgitator remembered 4ZZZ playing 'Task Force' constantly:

> So, if you listen to this song today you can hear the young Brisbane noise merchants kicking against the Joh-era police stormtroopers in this south-east Queensland classic.[9]

The Saints, with songs such as 'Brisbane (Security City)' and of course '(I'm) Stranded', ignited Australia's 'snot' punk explosion. Because no one would book them, they had to put on their own shows, which the police then raided, threatening to confiscate their instruments. Ed Kuepper reflects:

> I think the band was able to develop a more obnoxious demeanour, thanks to our surroundings, than had everyone been really nice. (Stafford, pp. 3)

Really nice was not, in fact, what everyone was being. Coming from a tradition of neo-pietism, an authoritarian philosophy that wedded religion to politics, Bjelke-Petersen spoke in the language of Christian corporatism. His Country Party – later the National Party – made Queensland safe for industrial and commercial exploitation. Business interests and State power walked hand-in-hand with God in the land of Joh. The Fitzgerald Inquiry into police corruption in Queensland (1987–1989)[10] would lead to Bjelke-Petersen's ousting in December 1987, although his party would stay in office for a further two years. For pretty much all of the Go-Betweens' first run, this regime was the power in their homeland. In April 2024, Brisbane's Woolloongabba Art Gallery mounted a show of Paul O'Brien's photographs to accompany *Nowhere Fast: Brisbane's Punk and Post-punk Scene 1978–1982*, which Robert Forster curated with John Willsteed. Robert recalled:

> There were people that gravitated to that and people that were horrified. It was at the time [of] the Joh Bjelke-Petersen government, so it was cracked down on, it was in no way understood, and it was seen as a threat to the government. There was just no tolerance for culture. The Queensland government and the powers that be had no comprehension

of what it was, but were aggressive against it at the same time, you know?[11]

As artistic youths growing up in that environment, Robert and Grant needed a core of resilience and self-confidence. In this town, to hear the Velvet Underground, you had to buy records by mail order from America or find a shop that imported them. Scarcity gave these cultural artefacts the cachet of secret knowledge. The sharing of LPs from beyond the horizon, handed on from friend to friend, must have imbued everything with more life, more intensity. The Irish poet Patrick Kavanagh wrote in 'Advent' (1942): 'We have tested and tasted too much, lover. / Through a chink too wide there comes in no wonder.'[12] His point, as well as celebrating Catholic abstemiousness, seems to anticipate the hypersaturated media deluge of our time, where nothing lingers in the memory for long, because there is so much *content* being released every day. Many people have developed a sense of entitlement to being entertained without having to work for it or pay for it. Cultural hunger keeps the taste buds piqued, and in Brisbane during the punk years, as in Ireland, there was relatively little to watch, to hear, to read. When you found something that spoke to you, it was golden.

Samuel Beckett, Jean-Luc Godard, The Monkees. Those touchstones fuelled the young Go-Betweens. Patti Smith, James Joyce, Creedence Clearwater Revival. Those, too. With the kind of enthusiasm which burns hotter in the young, these lovers of Jonathan Richman, Jean Genet and the Mamas and the Papas were steeped in a brew of influences discovered in suburbia. Through their experience of art, they saw the world beyond.

But who were these young men who would one day end up sword-fighting in the traffic after a drama history lesson at the off-campus theatre, an event later described by Robert as the first Go-Betweens performance?[13]

Here is a very potted history. Grant William McLennan, born in 1958 in Rockhampton, moved to Cairns with his family after his father, a doctor, died when Grant was four; and later to a cattle station in Far North Queensland when his mother remarried. A film-obsessed boy with a poetic sensibility, he was sent at age twelve to a conservative church boarding school in Brisbane. His father's early death and the isolation of five years in that school added to Grant's burden of childhood trauma and inspired his great song 'Cattle and Cane'. Meanwhile, Robert Derwent Garth Forster, born in 1957 in Brisbane, was raised in a happy family environment where he was looked after and encouraged. This crucial early difference in circumstances would form the intertwining roots of their relationship and shape how they grew around each other right to the end.

In what Robert has described as a 'Mick and Keith moment',[14] he and Grant met in 1976[15] during a theatre arts class while they studied English at the University of Queensland. Grant was carrying a copy of either Ian Hunter's eponymous first album or Ry Cooder's *Paradise and Lunch*.[16]

Tracey Thorn, who places the boys' meeting in 1977, calls it 'a real meet cute' and writes that Grant was carrying both records, as well as Jackson Browne's *Late for the Sky*.[17] Myths are made of such divergences.

When they met, Robert was in a band called the Godots. Grant was more into writing for *Cinema Papers*, working at the campus cinema, the Schonell and dreaming of being either a director or a great film critic. Robert told ABC News in a 2016 interview to mark ten years since Grant's death:

> I thought he was smart, he was attentive, he was one of the smarter people in the room. I came to the realisation that an artistic compatibility was more important than some sort of musical prowess. I'm writing these simple songs, and I said, 'Grant, I can teach you how to play the bass, and most of my songs are two, three chords, and I think, let's at least try'.[18]

'No', was the simple response. Robert continued in the Godots and wrote 'Karen'. Two chords, D and E minor. Grant attended a Battle of the Bands gig at the Academy of Music during which the Godots wowed the audience. When Robert gave him a tape and asked him again to start a band, Grant accepted in December 1977 by sending his friend a postcard which said, 'there's something there for the future. Anyway. Grant'.[19]

In May 1978, as the Go-Betweens, they recorded their first single, 'Lee Remick' and its B-side 'Karen', and released it through a small local Brisbane record company, the Able Label. In keeping with one of the genre's finest traditions, both are love songs to the unattainable. Robert's next song, 'People Say' develops the sound but retains the lyrical sentiment. Ian McFarlane describes the first two singles:

> they were sparsely produced, poorly played yet passionately performed folksy, post-punk pop songs. They were sunny,

catchy and hopelessly romantic, earning the band immediate local and international acclaim.[20]

Hopelessly romantic is right. Listening to their early music now and understanding who was making it, you can hear that for the Go-Betweens, rebellion came in the form of simply being themselves. This can be radical: a flower planted in the barrel of a gun, a lone student standing in front of a column of tanks, a folksinger going electric. The refusal to conform is a powerful act, and it should never be incumbent on a musician to shoehorn a message into a song. For one thing, to paraphrase Ed Kuepper, if you need to explain a work of art, it's not doing its job.

Grassroots protest songs tell truths that need to be told. They are essential in any society that, at least nominally, allows dissent and can be a lifeline in those that don't. The music of the Go-Betweens is to be found at a different point on the political spectrum, where the art itself is the protest rather than a vehicle for a manifesto. They were conscious of that, too; in an early interview, Robert and Grant criticized Dexys Midnight Runners for singing about passion rather than *being* passionate.[21]

Laurie Anderson, in her song 'Smoke Rings', ponders which is more macho, the pineapple or the knife.[22] That gets to the heart of the matter: it takes strength to endure. On the same wavelength, Pablo Picasso asked in 1945:

> What do you think an artist is? An imbecile who has only eyes? On the contrary, he's a political being, constantly alive to heart-rending, fiery, or happy events. Painting is not done to

decorate apartments. It is an instrument of war for attack and defence against the enemy.[23]

His thesis was proven in 2003, when US secretary of state Colin Powell was due to make a speech at the United Nations, 'justifying' George W. Bush and Tony Blair's invasion of Iraq. *Slate* reported:

> U.N. officials hung a blue curtain over a tapestry reproduction of Picasso's *Guernica* at the entrance of the Security Council. The spot is where diplomats and others make statements to the press, and ostensibly officials thought it would be inappropriate for Colin Powell to speak about war in Iraq with the twentieth century's most iconic protest against the inhumanity of war as his backdrop.[24]

Guernica, a response to the aerial bombardment of civilians during the Spanish Civil War, and a warning to our own time, is the kind of protest art that doesn't need a slogan.

* * *

On 26 May 2024, Robert Forster and I meet at his hotel in Bloomsbury, London. It's the morning after his second show at a venue called Omeara. Because he knew I'd be there, he says, he played several songs from *Danger in the Past*.

He cuts an elegant figure, not at all a typical rock star, whatever that means. He asks about the weathered leather satchel I carry, and when I say it was a gift from my wife, he replies, 'Yeah, whoever gave you that truly understands you'.

Robert suggests we walk and get a coffee, so we stroll to Ginger Jules' café in leafy Gordon Square and sit at a table outside. There, in the crisp summer air, over extra-hot lattes and sparkling spring water, we speak for an hour or so before he has to travel north to where his son Louis is playing at a festival. Among the subjects we discuss is one often overlooked by those who write history, the effect that political events have on the individual.

PC: Growing up in Brisbane during the Bjelke-Petersen period must have had an influence on who you became.

RF: That is true. I'd never thought of that. Especially, strangely enough, within families. Within my family. Because my grandparents, although we were sort of middle-class, working-class family, there were no labour or union leanings. My parents were conservative, not wealthy people. I think, at that time my family would have been very typical. I think it would have split families to an extent. It was a conservative, obviously corrupt [society], skewed by a gerrymandering dictatorship[25] that was obviously two-faced. It echoes, say, someone like Trump, where you go 'but can't you *see*'? It was like that, but it was a whole different thing. It wasn't as crazy, but it was like Christianity, fundamentalism, anti-intellectualism, all rolled into one. The police are on his side and are corrupted; there are deals being done. And so, within families that was difficult. And I was definitely someone who saw it a bit more with my father and my grandparents, though it never erupted into anything. But then when I went to Queensland University, it was the one bastion. The churches were for it [the regime], the newspaper [the *Courier Mail*] was for it, but the university was the one place where people talked openly and there was resistance. And I think the other thing really about this – which was also tied up with my family – I was that first generation who went to university. So, it was a little bit like my parents – classic story – people who are not wealthy, that take on second jobs to send their child to what we call a private school, which was public school here [in England]. I get educated, I'm going to university, so I have immediately a different political view. I've been educated out of my parents' milieu. And so that was bound up very much within the political system because Bjelke-Petersen was in power from 1969 to 1987. It was a twenty-year rule, and Queensland was the joke of Australia. So, he was ruling on the Bible and stacking the elections, and the police were his. Public demonstrations were banned. He provoked the radical left so that he could then turn to the people and go, you know, these people are communists; vote for me. It was a bizarre system. The fact that it happened in the middle of the twentieth century seems bizarre now. Horrible.

PC: Did this background influence your music at all?

RF: No. Oh. No. No. No.

PC: I didn't mean that you wrote directly political songs, but that the situation must have influenced your sensibility as an artist.

RF: This has been brought up, and I sort of say the fact that to write 'Lee Remick', to write 'Karen' in the middle of this, there was a rebellious act to it because it's just completely not addressing [the situation] and it's going to a sort of playful place, inspired by books and film. Intellectual but not in that way. The fact that even in that system, people like us can be produced and can create things like this, there's a rebellion, a rebellious act to that. It was so outrageous, you know, 'Karen' and 'Lee Remick', all of that, and it was grasped upon. People liked it because they could see that it was so incongruous to what was going on that it had its own power in a way.

PC: You and Grant were being yourselves despite everything.

RF: That's the key. We were being ourselves. Yes, that's it. Exactly right. And Grant and I recognized each other in the situation. A lot of people left. There were one or two at the show last night [at Omeara] who are Brisbane people, who left Brisbane in the late '70s – and, ah, it flushed people out. Because people who wanted to do anything creative, there was no infrastructure, because culture was completely not encouraged. It was all about mining and attacking the natural environment, it was all that, and so creative people left, and they went all around the world. Not even creative people, people who just went 'this is crazy'. And it looked, even in the '70s, like this was going to last another ten years. It looked really entrenched because the system was so skewered.

* * *

Lindy Morrison joined the Go-Betweens in 1980, fulfilling Robert and Grant's idea of the perfect structure for a pop group: either two men and a woman, or two women and a man. Lindy's drumming would become the third essential element in their sound.

Seven years their senior, Belinda 'Lindy' Morrison (born 1951 in Brisbane) had been the drummer for the post-punk band Zero since 1978, in which she played alongside Irena Luckus, John Willsteed (a future Go-Between) and others. Having come out of an older counterculture, Lindy had spent years working as an advocate for Indigenous Australians' rights, had been active in the politics of feminism, and had travelled adventurously in Europe. She famously called this configuration of the band 'two wimps and a witch'; *Two Wimps and a Witch* had been mooted as a title for the band's first album until Lindy suggested *Send Me a Lullaby* instead, inspired by Zelda Fitzgerald's novel *Save Me the Waltz*.[26]

Whereas Lindy and Robert would become a couple, the relationship between her and Grant was fractious, a tension that nonetheless fit the idea of the Go-Betweens as a gang like the one in Truffaut's *Jules et Jim*, or Godard's *Bande à Part*.[27] That second title is derived from the phrase 'faire bande à parte', in English meaning 'to stand out from the crowd'.

In conversation with John Willsteed at Brisbane's Avid Reader bookshop on 9 November 2009, Robert remembered the trio's early days.

> The first show that the Go-Betweens ever played in Sydney at the Paris Theatre in 1980 . . . The bill for this night was the Go-Betweens on first, the Laughing Clowns on second, and the Birthday Party on third. It was a great bill. We'd actually headed down by train – Lindy, Grant, myself – and we went to the back of the Paris Theatre. We didn't know anyone and we sat in the stalls in the darkness and watched the Birthday Party and the Laughing Clowns soundcheck. We were completely spooked. We just wanted to crawl out of that theatre and get back on the train and come back to Brisbane.[28]

Needless to say, they overcame those jitters. Inspired by Bob Dylan's 'thin wild mercury sound', Robert and Grant developed their own songwriting style, which came to be known as 'that striped sunlight sound'[29]. With the arrival of Robert Vickers on bass in 1982, and Amanda Brown on violin, keyboards, guitar and oboe in 1986, their definitive line-up of the 1980s was established.

The Go-Betweens may not have needed to storm the barricades, but they did want to storm the charts. Yet they never forgot where they came from. To paraphrase a later song, 'Surfing Magazines', its lyrics reflecting on his youth, Robert and his band apart would try 'to be the kind of people the authorities can't reach'.

Eventually, the authorities – under new management – came to honour them. When Brisbane City Council held a public vote in 2009 to christen the city's new bridge, they named it after the Go-Betweens.[30]

3 Love is a sign

In the annals of romance, not many love stories have been ignited by a bout of Rocky Mountain Spotted Fever. On 10 May 1989, Bill Berry, R.E.M.'s drummer, came down with that tick-borne infection, and the show at Circus Krone in Munich was cancelled an hour before door time. The Go-Betweens had opened for R.E.M. at Phillipshalle in Dusseldorf the night before but tonight found themselves at a loose end.

Karin Bäumler and her friends had come to see Robert's band, two years after he had first met her at a Go-Betweens show in Heidelberg. Since that gig, their mutual attraction had blossomed quietly. Now they received the gift of a free evening to spend together while the others partied.[1]

There was much suffering to come for poor Bill Berry, and R.E.M. had to cancel the next three shows: 12 May, PC 69, Bielefeld; 13 May, Kongresshalle, Frankfurt; 14 May, Grosse Feiheit 36, Hamburg. This meant that Robert and Karin were free to drive the 127 kilometres to her shared house in Alteglofsheim, a village in the Regensburg district of Bavaria, for a few days.

At some point during their tryst, Karin put on Robert's dress. This was the dress that Grant suggested Robert wear at their record industry showcase in LA on the *16 Lovers Lane* tour. It had shocked John Fagot, VP of Promotion for Capitol Records, into deciding that the Go-Betweens' American career was over before it had begun.² Never mind that R.E.M.'s Michael Stipe, a son of Athens, Georgia, also wore dresses. A few years later, Kurt Cobain and Evan Dando would be celebrated for doing the same – belatedly following the lead of David Bowie. His 'man-dress', by designer Mr Fish,³ adorned him on the UK cover of *The Man Who Sold the World*, as well as on his 1971 tour of the US. Mick Jagger had beaten Bowie to it, wearing a different design by Mr Fish, a white, puffy-sleeved 'dress for men', at the Rolling Stones' 1969 Hyde Park gig. For Robert, the dress came naturally. He'd had it made because, he said,

> it saved me going into thrift shops and it stopped me having to ask for a dress for my girlfriend who happens to be the same size and height as me.⁴

In *Grant & I*, Robert describes the moment when Karin asked to see the dress in his hotel room after the first cancelled R.E.M. gig. In *The Go-Betweens: Right Here*, Kriv Stenders' film about the band, he remembers:

> The epilogue to the dress is that when I moved in with Karin, I spent four days with her. And I don't know whether it was her or me, but it was like, oh why don't you try it on? And so, Karin put on the dress, and it fit her like a glove. She just looked amazing in it. So, it was this bizarre thing where I had the dress made for myself and I was wearing it and then the woman I had fallen in love with, she was wearing the dress.⁵

Asked if he ever wore the dress after that, Robert replied, 'No, it had found its home.'⁶

Who wouldn't take that as a sign? It may not have been a glass slipper, but it was close, and it makes for a powerful moment to mark the start of a new relationship. The normality of their situation didn't stop whispers in Australia from turning Karin into a German princess whose father owned a brewery. In his song 'German Farmhouse', Robert would describe this period fondly – drinking beer, smoking cigarettes, listening to country music and contentedly putting on a little weight – but for all the picturesque details recounted in the fairytale legend of Alteglofsheim, this was a home, not a fortress. The stars had aligned, that's all.

If you were so inclined, you could read Germany's political transformation as a further indication that the wider world endorsed this small human story, a hill of beans envied by mountains.[7] The Berlin Wall would fall. East and West would be united. In that moment of change, hope was not only infectious, it was beautiful.

By the time of the next Go-Betweens show, a headliner at Govan Town Hall in Glasgow on 15 May, Robert and Karin were an item, which meant that he had to end his relationship with his girlfriend Kathleen Phillips, for whom he had composed the song 'Rock'n'Roll Friend'.[8] He did so by writing to her from the road, balancing his feelings of cowardice against the self-assurance that Karin was the one for him. Contrary to Leonard Cohen's song, true love does leave traces.[9]

At the end of the European leg of R.E.M.'s tour to play rescheduled dates, the Go-Betweens returned to Munich on 29 June. Robert met Karin again, and this time they drove off together for good. It was his thirty-second birthday.

Karin, a violinist in the band Baby You Know, shared the house at Alteglofsheim with fellow band member Erhard Grundl (later a Green Party politician representing Bavaria in the Bundestag) and another student called Kerstin. Robert would play on Baby You Know's debut and produce their 1992 album, *Clear Water*. Some tracks on that record sound like the early Go-Betweens, although the one Robert composed, 'I Love You Still', sounds like Mazzy Star.

Danger in the Past could be said to have begun in that house, as it was there, in this very different setting, that Robert wrote new songs: 'Danger in the Past', 'Is This What You Call Change', 'I've Been Looking for Somebody', 'Dear Black Dream'... A real maturity had entered his lyrics, following on from the more open-hearted direction he had been taking on *16 Lovers Lane*. Three of Robert's songs on that album feel especially personal: 'Love Is a Sign', 'Clouds' and 'Dive for Your Memory'.

Late in 1989, the Go-Betweens started regrouping to make their next album. The rest of the band had gone back to Sydney while Robert remained, for now, in his Bavarian idyll. Grant was given the job of sacking John Willsteed, who had replaced Robert Vickers on bass in 1987, after *Tallulah*. Willsteed had been partying hard on the road, as had the rest of them, but he didn't seem inclined to stop.[10]

Amanda Brown recalls that John Willsteed didn't even like the music of the band he was in.[11] That said, his virtuoso playing on their 1988 album *16 Lovers Lane*, including the flamenco-inflected guitar solo on 'Streets of Your Town', is undeniable.

John Willsteed's departure was only the first non-amicable split in the line-up. In *Right Here*, he almost tears up at the memory of this period, recalling 'Dive for Your Memory' as one spectacular recording he feels lucky to have had a hand in creating. In 2024, having long since entered the groves of academe, Dr John Willsteed was awarded the John Oxley Fellowship for his fascinating interview project named after that song, *Dive for Your Memory – Queensland music stories*.[12] One of his interview subjects is Robert Forster.

Down to a four-piece, the Go-Betweens went ahead with plans to make their new album. Robert says he now appreciates the polished, luxuriant sound of *16 Lovers Lane*, but after its commercial failure, he wanted to go in a different direction altogether. Grant, too, found it frustrating that even with such a beautifully made record, they couldn't get a hit. 'Streets of Your Town' had received three weeks of A-list airplay on BBC Radio 2, but Beggars Banquet didn't have the resources to put into promotion and capitalize on the opportunity.[13] Rather than the smash it could have been, the single brushed the upper reaches of the charts then slipped away.

At Robert's apartment on Botany Street, Bondi Junction, he and Grant put down about twenty-eight songs between 24 and 25 October. They had brought Tony Cohen up from Melbourne with his four-track to record the demos, as Robert and Grant sang and played guitar while sitting across from each other.

Cohen, part of the ex-pat Australian scene in London half a decade earlier, had produced and engineered records for the Boys Next Door, the Birthday Party and the Bad Seeds and had also co-produced the Go-Betweens' debut album *Send Me a Lullaby*. He was likely to be sympathetic with the stripped-back direction in which the two songwriters were planning to go. And so it proved. Robert, listening back to the recordings of the sessions with Cohen, realized that this was a new tone, a new feeling. He and Grant were:

> moving away from the angular rock and pop that had once inspired them and into their own classic singer-songwriter territory.[14]

According to Robert, Grant's best new songs, from a wide selection, were 'Easy Come Easy Go', 'The Day My Eyes Came Back', 'Haunted House', 'Broadway Bride' and 'Dream About Tomorrow'. Four of these would end up on Grant's *Watershed*, and 'The Day My Eyes Came Back' would appear on its follow-up, *Fireboy*. As for his own songs, he reflected,

> I had four that I thought were keepers, good enough for an album – 'Is This What You Call Change', 'I've Been Looking For Somebody', 'Dear Black Dream' and 'Danger in the Past'. The latter the jewel in my crown.[15]

When thinking about a producer for this new Go-Betweens album, Tony Cohen was in the picture after a number of candidates had been considered but ruled out. Grant had proposed Hal Willner, but when Robert visited him in New York that August, although they got on exceptionally well, he found that Willner's approach would not be suitable: 'his speciality as a producer was esoteric solo artists like Marianne Faithfull and Gavin Friday'.[16] Robert also flirted with:

> the mad idea of getting Sydney painter Brett Whiteley involved. Had anyone in the world made an album produced by a

famous artist since Warhol did the first Velvet Underground LP?[17]

Lindy and Amanda suggested one of the producers who had recently worked on *Tin Machine II*, but for Robert, although he adored Bowie, 'Pixies-style rock . . . was not the direction our songs were taking us'.[18]

In the practice room, with new bassist Michael Armiger on board as well as Lindy and Amanda, it became clear that the latest songs did not fit the group. Lindy referred to the evolving record as Robert's album – more folky – whereas she and Amanda were thinking of going in a more electronic direction. Musical differences are often given as the reason for a band breaking up. In the case of the Go-Betweens, it was certainly one of them, as Amanda and Grant were now working together on songs. Amanda says in *Right Here*:

> I was never an intentional focus puller. Increasingly, Grant and I were foregrounded. Because we lived together it was inevitable that our creativity meshed. The focus had changed. Robert was pushed to the side, a position he'd have hated.[19]

Lindy Morrison had given much to the Go-Betweens' sound but with a few exceptions rock culture at the time tended to underestimate the talent of drummers. In *My Rock'n'Roll Friend*, a memoir of her longstanding friendship with Lindy, Tracey Thorn writes:

> The Go-Betweens are one of those bands who are reviewed largely on the strength of their lyrics, as though they have published a volume of poetry rather than made an album.

The music is mentioned less often than the words, and the drumming least of all. If writers struggle to write about music, then drumming leaves them stumped.[20]

Bernard Zuel, a journalist who has for a long time written about the Go-Betweens and their members' solo careers, observed in the *Sydney Morning Herald*:

> the seemingly fractured but actually constructed and essential patterns of both Lindy Morrison's drums and her intellectual input to the hot-housed fervour of two boys from Brisbane. There is never enough written about how important Morrison was to the Go-Betweens; she wasn't their first person on drums, but she was the drummer who made them *this* band.[21]

Grant McLennan himself acknowledged what Lindy Morrison brought to the recording of 'Cattle and Cane':

> It had a great rhythm which I don't think any drummer in the world could've played except her. That rhythm never ceases to amaze me.[22]

The group had hired Amanda Brown having seen her play in a café. A multi-instrumentalist, she'd already enjoyed an impressive career in music, notably with the Sydney jazz-rock combo Climbing Frame and had trained in classical ballet. Her oboe on 'Bye Bye Pride' makes it soar. Her violin on 'The Clarke Sisters' elevates it with a plaintive touch of mystery. Glenn Smith, writing in the *Toppermost* blog,[23] noted:

> Amanda Brown brought a new and dynamic sophistication to the songwriting and arrangements. Amanda and Grant started

a relationship, thereby creating two partnerships in the band, which brought a different feel to McLennan's lyrics, there was a new poignancy and focus to his words, his pictures being painted with one person in mind.

Discussing his curation of the second Go-Betweens box set in 2020, Robert told Paula Farr of Silent Radio in the UK:

> The highlight for me was hearing how we improved as songwriters and improved as a band. And with the addition of Amanda Brown, primarily on violin, it enhanced our live sound. In the process becoming a much more dynamic group on stage. We could all feel a new power we had.[24]

There is one song on which all four – Forster, McLennan, Morrison and Brown – share writing credits: 'Doo-Wop in A', a B-side from the *Tallulah* sessions. An enjoyable homage to the girl-group sound of the 1960s, its lyrics serve as an answer to 'Karen', from the point of view of the librarian. Lindy and Amanda take the vocals, with the refrain: 'Just got over loving him.'

Much has been written about how the Go-Betweens ended. 'I could list 20 or 30 reasons why the band needed to break up', Robert told the *Sydney Morning Herald*.[25] 'The simplest being that Grant told me he wanted to leave.' The article goes on:

> They broke the news to the female members of the band simultaneously. Forster informed Morrison, who was apoplectic about the premeditated break-up. McLennan informed his companion Brown. She unceremoniously dumped him.

Factor in Amanda and Grant's romantic relationship, as well as Lindy's history with Robert, and this was an emotional as well as a professional bombshell that the two men dropped. Amanda recalls in *Right Here*:

> The night Grant told me that he and Robert were going to go off and make their acoustic record without the rest of the band I pretty much immediately packed up a suitcase and left. Because it really did feel like everything went into freefall and defence mechanisms had to be erected. And I suddenly had to work out what to do with my life because I didn't have a job anymore and in fact everything just imploded spectacularly because Grant turned around and said he'd do anything he could to make things right again. By that stage it was too late because things were so broken. The trust had gone, and I couldn't face going back to that.[26]

In the same interview, sitting beside Amanda, Lindy says:

> I think it's been substantial for our individual careers that this happened to us, because it made us seriously want to make a mark. Both of us refused to be defined as the girlfriends and that's what they did when they dumped us. They treated us like ex-wives and that was the greatest insult.[27]

Grant, having never considered that Amanda might leave, went into a terrible decline. Robert took care to check up on him every day, fearful that any visit might find Grant dead, until after a week or two, the storm clouds grew less ominous.

On 17 January 1990, Robert flew out to Germany to be with Karin.

Still heartbroken, Grant soon decided that instead of the folk duo album, he wanted to make a solo record and have Amanda play on it, in the fond hope of restoring their relationship. Although she would eventually perform on *Watershed*, their romantic life together was over, and everyone except Grant knew it.

Perhaps welcoming the distraction, he also made the first of two Jack Frost albums with Steve Kilbey around this time. Kilbey founded the Church, whose album *Starfish* achieved the kind of chart appeal that had eluded the Go-Betweens, with the hit song 'Under the Milky Way'. For the Church, their commercial success had come as a result of handing themselves over to American producers Greg Ladanyi and Waddy Wachtel. The song struck a vein of gold with the public, initially to the chagrin of Kilbey, who saw it as just another one of the hundreds he'd written, but it has endured. Chris Gibson notes in his book on *Starfish*:

> In Australia especially, 'Milky Way' became canonical – an unofficial 'alternative' national anthem (implying the southern cross constellation on the national flag), alongside 'Wide Open Road' by the Triffids and 'Cattle and Cane' by the Go-Betweens.[28]

The friendship between Kilbey and McLennan and its heroin-related fate is a story for another book, which Steve Kilbey has written: his memoir, *Something Quite Peculiar*.[29]

In terms of songwriting, Grant was nothing if not prolific, but this could mean quantity at the expense of quality, with more songs pouring out of him than he perhaps knew what to do with. His decision to go solo, which manager Bob Johnson relayed in a phone call to Robert, seemed like a betrayal.[30] Although Grant apologized a couple of weeks later for reneging on their agreement to work as a duo, this turn of events convinced Robert that now was the time to make his own album.

It would be a decade before Grant and Robert recorded again as the Go-Betweens, with the addition of new bandmembers.[31] They would have several live reunions during the period now known as the intermission, notably supporting Lloyd Cole on tour in 1991;[32] and for the tenth anniversary of French music and politics magazine *Les Inrockuptibles* in 1996.[33] Among the aliases mooted for their various reconnections, 'The Australian Go-Betweens' drily sent up the burgeoning tribute-band genre that featured acts such as the Australian Doors and the Australian Pink Floyd.

Above all, they remained friends even as their early solo records bore witness to the different courses their lives took. Robert's albums shine with love songs to Karin, whom he married in May 1990. Grant's own songs are ripe with longing for the woman he had lost and would never get back.

In the light of that Bavarian spring, Robert Forster, solo artist, had the songs he needed for his album. It was time to go into the studio.

4 Intermission

Robert Forster's debut feels like a breakthrough record. Not just in terms of his music but his life. It stands within that tradition of revelatory solo albums made by people who have just left a band that had previously defined them. Bob Mould's *Workbook* (1989), Bjork's *Debut* (1993), Natalie Merchant's *Tigerlily* (1995), John Grant's *Queen of Denmark* (2010) – any number of artists whose creativity has been either nurtured or compromised within their group surroundings have burst forth in a glorious solo release. Robert recognizes this in his own first album.

PC: Would you say that *Danger in the Past* is a coming-of-age album?

RF: Yes, that's very perceptive. It was. I think it coincided with a number of changes within me, probably as a person – definitely as a person – and as a writer and I think there were reflected in it changes in my life. Obviously, the break-up of the Go-Betweens is a period of change because the band had been going since 1978 and really it had governed my life totally. It governed Grant's life, and it governed the lives of anyone that joined – Lindy, everyone. And so, for it to suddenly break – even if I'd have gone off and become a baker or worked in some other way, it would have been a momentous change – and it was. And because I stayed a singer-songwriter, I think it all went into my work.

PC: After the break-up of the band, with Grant in such a bad way, you had to step up and become the older brother to your friend. How do you now see that time?

RF: In hindsight, it seemed like it had to be. And also – you know people expect there to be two reasons for the break-up of the Go-Betweens. There's about a hundred. And I think – he was the one that said it in the moment. The practice room was very difficult. There were tensions in the band. It wasn't a pleasant place to be. And it stopped being enjoyable. And that was thrown into greater relief for me in that I'd spent the summer in Germany with Karin, and I'd seen another way of life. I'd spent three months with her from June to September, a golden summer in Bavaria, and then I went back to Sydney to this dysfunctional band that was like, 'oh my god'. And then I immediately left for another three weeks, to get out. The practice room was impossible, and Grant was the one who said, 'I want to leave, I want the band to stop, I want to leave'. So that was that. But I think then, how it then twisted over the next month was a nightmare and Grant came out of it really badly. And I had somewhere to go to, to be with someone, and, um, there was a big difference there, a huge difference, and how all of that played out. I always wondered just how he thought it was going to go, but whatever calculation he made, it was completely wrong.

PC: You were going through this turmoil too, even with the security of your life with Karin. Did your songs change as they moved from one setting to another, or was it obvious that there was a new kind of energy in this material?

RF: The thing was, it never really got tested because the songs I wrote in that summer – this was something that I didn't really see – the band couldn't play them. We couldn't play

'Danger in the Past' – because I wrote it and I realized it was like nothing I'd ever written. It was a six-verse folk ballad basically, and we were a rock band. We tried to play 'I've Been Looking for Somebody', and it didn't work. You know, I wasn't writing four to the floor, not necessarily rock'n'roll, but rock'n'roll or pop or whatever. I didn't really have any songs like that. And so, we ended up rehearsing sort of second-tier material that I had, one was called 'Running the Risk of Losing You' which was a lot more old-style. And the band could grasp onto that, particularly Lindy; she could understand that. But 'I've Been Looking for Somebody', she didn't play that. 'Danger in the Past' was twelve-string guitars and bass, so that would have cracked the band anyway because when you listen to all of our records, there's virtually no song without drums and so we didn't really test the material. The band never played 'Baby Stones'; the band never played 'Danger in the Past'. The band tried to play 'I've Been Looking for Somebody'. I'd written 'Is This What You Call Change' – again, not a song with drums. And so, I was writing material that didn't fit the band I was in, which was a very strange situation but there it was.

PC: It seems that the music itself was showing you the future.

RF: Yeah. But I was still in the band. You know, it was like, how do we sort this out? And that's another reason why the band broke up. There was no plan. Every album that we made, there was always a plan. And we all went through it together. It was always fairly, you know, 'We're gonna make *Liberty Belle* with Richard Preston'. Or – we're not gonna have a producer, we want to do it ourselves. And we're gonna do that. And then that worked – we're gonna do *Tallulah* – we really like Richard, we like working in London, we're gonna do it with him, OK, everyone's just on a mission. And then

Mark Wallis mixes *Tallulah*, he completely – it's unique what he does to our sound, let's make an album with Mark. He makes *16 Lovers Lane*. Everyone's for it. Go! The next one, which was gonna be *Freakchild*, there was no consensus. Even before we got in the practice room, everyone had a different idea. It was the first time we never had a common idea. Yeah. And so, here's reason number 58 why the record fell down. And why, you know, why it didn't happen.

Another Country

5 A ballroom in Berlin

Recording for *Danger in the Past* took place from 20 June to 4 July 1990, mainly at Hansa Studio II, the Meistersaal, on Köthener Strasse. Situated between Potsdamer Platz and the now-fallen Berlin Wall, the studio had hosted sessions for David Bowie's *Low* and *"Heroes"*, David Sylvian's *Brilliant Trees*, three Bad Seeds albums and many others.

Musically as well as geopolitically, there was a lot going on in West Berlin that year. Bowie, taking time off from Tin Machine, had brought his *Sound+Vision* greatest hits tour to the city in April. Roger Waters was about to unleash his presentation of *The Wall* at the Brandenburg Gate. U2 would be along in October to work on *Achtung, Baby*. The Irish group would find the studio not up to spec for their purposes, and its use as a ballroom during the Nazi period made them uneasy.[1] Nonetheless, they would write and record their anthem 'One' in this room, as a response to tensions within the band. The fact that U2 stayed at Hansa for only two songs rather than the entirety of *Achtung, Baby*, makes *Danger in the Past* possibly the last full rock album recorded in Studio II before it was returned to its former use as a performance space. With Germany about to reunite, the fate of the Meistersaal, which dated from 1910, was just another small eddy in the currents of change that were swirling around.

Robert had come here in the spirit of that earlier version of Bowie, the one who had run off with Iggy Pop on their emigré bohemian adventure. Calling on Mick Harvey to produce, especially to work in this great hall, was a masterstroke. Harvey had co-founded the Birthday Party and the Bad Seeds. He was also a member of Crime and the City Solution, whose new album, *Paradise Discotheque*, would be released on the same day as *Danger in the Past*. As de facto musical director and business manager of the Bad Seeds, Mick Harvey had a lot of plates spinning but none interfered with his production duties now.

Harvey enlisted Thomas Wydler of the Bad Seeds to play drums, and Robert brought in Hugo Race, a former Bad Seed, for guitar overdubs, having met him in a bar on the first night and suggested him to Mick. Sensitive to the needs of the music, this group helped Robert to achieve a 'pure Forster' sound.

The first day was all set up, with no recordings, as Mick and Robert took care to get the room just how they wanted it, placing mics optimally, considering the studio itself as a musical instrument and fine-tuning it to meet their needs.

The sessions went briskly, the speed at which the musicians worked offering creative freedom. No record company executive was there to insist that Robert use a DX7 or that Thomas slap gated reverb on his drums. In so many ways, it was no longer the 1980s.

Preparations had begun in earnest when Robert phoned Mick in Berlin, with the intention to make a record live in the studio, fast and clean, like artists he admired used to do in the 1960s. In Harvey, who has said he thinks this is how all records should be made, Robert had found a sympathetic producer.[2] In Victor Van Vugt, who had lately helmed the boards for Nick Cave and the Bad Seeds' *The Good Son*, on which Mick Harvey had played, he had found the ideal engineer. Van Vugt would go on to produce Robert's 2019 album *Inferno* and mix 2023's *The Candle and the Flame*.

Thomas Wydler was a member of the German experimental post-punk band Die Haut before joining the Bad Seeds. Of the *Danger in the Past* sessions, he recalls:

> **TW:** Well, I remember the recordings were only us three – Robert, Mick and me – in the great-sounding Hansa studio, the big old ballroom on the first floor. The engineer was Victor Van Vugt. Mick played bass, guitar, piano, percussion and possibly backing vocals. I met Robert when Die Haut played together with the Go-Betweens live in Europe. We had a powerful, good time![3]

Hansa was a significant change from the studios Robert had been used to recording in, one he appears to have relished:

> You're not in a tin shed in Camden, because you believe in yourself, and you put the budget into the room.[4]

That budget was well spent, and in these grander surroundings, the musicians worked simply but effectively:

> Thomas would listen to a demo; Mick, on bass, would talk him through the arrangement; we'd go into the recording room, play the song no more than four times, do a take, and then go on to the next number.[5]

While discussing his albums with *Uncut*, Robert named *Danger in the Past* as a personal favourite, and described how the recording sessions went:

> In Hansa, you don't have to double-track an electric guitar, everything's so big. It's a sound that goes back to Buddy Holly's records or to *Highway 61* – there are no overdubs on those records. We did it in 12 days, recorded and mixed, with Hugo Race, Thomas Wydler and Mick – a very tight crew – and it was a beautiful experience.[6]

Hansa was founded as a recording entity in 1965 when the Meisel brothers, Thomas and Peter, rented Ariola's Sonopress facility at Köthener Strasse. In 1975, having established Hansa I, the brothers bought the building and took possession of the Meistersaal, turning it into Hansa II. A curious blend of old and new, the music recorded here included Schlager songs, film soundtracks and classical music, as well as new wave and electronica. Bowie's time at Hansa is well documented. Hansa Tonstudios embodied the interzone spirit of West Berlin, an island of radical individualism in the heart of a divided Germany. Attractive to artists because it was relatively cheap to record there and the acoustics were phenomenal, Hansa had something else going for it: the city's feeling of being a small patch of light ripped out of the Iron Curtain. Now, to borrow a phrase from Alfred Hitchcock, this was a torn curtain. As the fall of the Berlin Wall signalled a new future for Germany, uncertain but hopeful, it seems appropriate that Robert recorded *Danger in the Past* only 150 metres away from where history itself had apparently just ended.[7]

When the Go-Betweens came to West Berlin in 1987, Robert had taken the opportunity to visit Hansa II. Exploring the studio space without his bandmates, he'd told himself that one day he would come back and make a record in the Meistersaal. Now here he was again, fulfilling his promise.

6 Hansa memories

I interviewed Mick Harvey in July 2024 via email, having attended his show at Omeara in London the night after seeing Robert play there. The two old friends and collaborators had passed each other in this city of the new Tories, four decades after having lived and worked here during the Thatcher years.

Mick was just back from his tour with Amanda Acevedo in support of his new album, *Five Ways to Say Goodbye*, when we discussed the recording sessions for *Danger in the Past*.

PC: How did you become involved in producing *Danger in the Past*, and what was your reaction to being asked?

MH: Robert contacted me and asked if I would be interested to produce the album with him. Of course, I was very interested. I had been a fan of Robert's writing since the first time I saw the Go-Betweens.

PC: Robert was going into the studio for the first time without his old band, including Grant McLennan. Was it part of your task to provide stability – like a musical director – or was that not a factor?

MH: Grant's absence was not a factor or an issue for me. I'd been asked to work with Robert on his songs, and that was the only thing which was in front of me as a task. I don't think Robert was asking for stability, though he may have been in need of some, considering he was on unfamiliar ground and without his usual support network. But it was only ever going to happen naturally – through the processes of working together as he gained confidence in what was happening.

PC: These recordings sound like they found their natural breathing space quickly, beautifully crafted but not overcooked. Did you work briskly because of time constraints, or because it gave the songs a certain freshness?

MH: First, we demoed the songs in a small studio in Kreuzberg. I think we did that in two days, so it was a case of finding a first idea together and going with it. Fortunately, most of those ideas were good, so there is a spontaneity evident from that which carried over into the basic tracks. Also, once we recorded the songs properly in Hansa, it was recorded live with myself, Robert and Thomas Wydler playing together, so it has a live and lively feel to the basic recordings which is often lost when recording one instrument at a time as, I understand, the three previous Go-Betweens albums had been done.

PC: The music on the album is evocative and atmospheric, unusually organic for its time. What approach did you take in the studio: setting up, recording takes and so on? Were you involved in engineering and mixing?

MH: The organic thing probably comes from the live playing approach but would also be to do with the sound of the hall at Hansa, which was a beautiful acoustic in which to work. One can really feel the room. I was not involved with the engineering but, as with most records I was doing at the time, I was very much hands on deck with the engineer in the mixing phase.

PC: Can you recall how the sessions went – was there a daily work routine, a set goal or was it looser than that?

MH: I can't remember exactly, but I would guess we had four or five days and twelve songs or something like that and would have aimed to do two or three basic tracks a day.

PC: With Thomas Wydler and Hugo Race taking part in the sessions as well as Karin and Robert, how did the group dynamic operate, and was there a particular division of labour, that is, an integrated band set-up or more a solo artist plus collaborators?

MH: As described, the basic tracks were with Thomas Wydler on drums, me on bass or keys (I guess) and Robert on guitar. I'm pretty sure all Hugo's parts were overdubbed and Karin's as well. There were a couple of songs with no drums, so I guess Robert and I just did those as a duo. Most of the drum parts were worked out by me in the demos, and Thomas sticks fairly close to the original rhythm ideas and drum patterns, so we must have rehearsed that before entering the studio.

PC: Did living and recording in West Berlin at that moment in history influence the record? How was it working at Hansa and at Preußen Tonstudios?

MH: I'm not sure if the West Berlin ambience influenced the record or not. I was living and recording there for years, so for me it probably seeped into everything a little bit, but it's probably hard for me to identify just how. For Robert, there may have been some specific feel he experienced. To work at Hansa was always a joy – such an amazing space. Preußenton was where we overdubbed and mixed and was also a good studio but just on that practical level.

PC: Did the experience of producing *Danger in the Past* give anything to your own practice as an artist?

MH: Of course, every project informs your practice and brings experiences from which you learn. I brought the experience

I had gained from working through the 1980s, during which time I had learnt a lot about arrangement and production. I think I entered the studio fairly determined to be in control of the production and arrangements in response, somehow, to my perception of where the Go-Betweens had ended up. I was on some kind of a mission there. In hindsight, I should, or perhaps could, have been more flexible and listening even more closely to Robert than I did, but I don't think the end result was compromised by that at all. It's just something I learnt through that experience.

PC: Robert, on his book tour, signed my copy of *Danger in the Past*: 'A classic'. How do you think the album holds up today, and do you have a favourite track, or any memories you'd like to share?

MH: Memories? Favourite tracks . . . no, not my thing. But I agree with Robert that it's a classic.

***

When I mentioned it to him in London, Robert seemed pleased to hear that Mick Harvey was in town and that they were playing the same venue, albeit a night apart, as their tour itineraries crossed. Speaking of Mick, we turned to the recordings at Hansa.

PC: *Danger in the Past* came out of Germany in a way because you found your new life there. Did you just call up Mick Harvey and say, 'Hi, would you produce my record?'

RF: Yeah. I mean, Mick had been a friend for a long time, and I knew that he would just – I loved what he'd done with the Bad Seeds and the Birthday Party. So sonically he was right in the park. And I knew he was someone I could work with. And I knew he would bring no preconceptions to the sound. He would be like – what do the songs need? I knew from those Bad Seeds records they were cutting live, which was a big thing with me; it was where I wanted to move to. Which I couldn't drag the Go-Betweens to. And so, I just contacted him from Bavaria. Also, he was living in Berlin at that time. And I said, 'you know the band's broken up, and I'd like to make a record with you'. He said he was very interested and said, 'Come up to Berlin'. This would have been March, April.

PC: By that stage, you knew about Grant's decision to go solo.

RF: I knew I was going to make the album in late January because Grant had contacted Beggars [Banquet, the Go-Betweens' record company] and told them that he was wanting to make a solo album. Then Bob [Johnson, manager] phoned me and said, 'Do you know?' I went 'no, what?' because I thought Grant and I were making an album. He had material that would have fitted the half that I had. If we had taken a completely different approach and gone, 'it's you and me', we need a bass player, we could have made an album. Actually, he could have played bass. He and I could have made an album. Because he had some songs – there were songs that were traditional Go-Betweens songs, but he also had other material. And he contacted Beggars and said he wanted to make a solo album.

PC: That must have been a shock. Was it then you started thinking about making a solo album?

RF: Beggars said that I could [make my album], so I phoned Mick. And he said, 'come up and play me some songs'. Which I thought was really cool – it wasn't just yes. I went up there and I played him probably about seven of the songs. In a studio. From memory, he might have played some bass on them or a bit of guitar. He was like, 'this is great, let me think about it, and I'll get in contact with you'. We talked about two weeks later. He went, 'I'm up for it, let's do it, great. Late June, how does that suit you?' I went, 'great'. And I said, 'where do you think we should record?' And he said Hansa. And I went, 'that was just – that's where I wanted to do it'. I wanted to do it in a big studio, and I'd been to Hansa on this trip I'd made there to Berlin in '87.

PC: Now you were back there, and it was actually going to happen.

RF: To me, this was like, I'm in my dream studio, and I'm actually walking into a record where it's not six weeks of extraordinarily hard work piecing together an album. I'm gonna walk in with songs like a singer-songwriter from the '60s and '70s. Just walk in, there are the musicians, let's record. And it was in Hansa, it was with Mick, it was perfect. It was absolutely the dream situation for me, even though it was completely insecure, it was what I wanted. I was very lucky.

PC: At that point, you were thinking of going in a looser direction with the music and not having it layer upon layer in terms of production. That kind of 'get in, do it, get out' vibe seems to suit the record.

RF: Yeah, that's what I wanted. Very much so. That's why you needed a room as big as Hansa. It's like – it's the reason why The Beatles recorded in Abbey Road, or Dylan recorded in Columbia Studios. You see those photos of Dylan cutting *Highway 61*; the studio's huge, the microphones are incredible. It's really, it's just a band; it's not layered. If it's recorded really well and it's big and it's got the punch, it'll work. You can have drums, bass, two guitars and it can sound huge. And that's what I wanted. I knew there wouldn't be much instrumentation, but I wanted to have this size and reverb and big sound, which is where the engineer Victor Van Vugt comes in; he was the other vital thing, because Victor I'd also known. Victor and Mick I'd known; Mick I'd known longer from Melbourne in the early '80s, from 1980 actually, so I knew Victor and he'd worked with the Bad Seeds, he'd worked with the Pogues and stuff. So, I knew he was right. And he was hanging around Berlin too. I knew that if I had a big studio with a good engineer, the record would sound really good.

PC: Did the scale of the room help that? I can imagine the acoustics must have been amazing.

RF: Incredible. Incredible. It was a very big, high-ceilinged room with windows. It was so big there was a stage in it, you know, right up one side. It was like a church cathedral, is the only way to describe it. So, you just strummed a guitar, and it was monstrous.

PC: The size of the recording space seems to have suited the size of the album. Previously, you were contributing five songs to an album, but now you had ten.

RF: Yeah, yeah. That was another breakthrough. You know, I felt like I was telling the whole story. And there was a story to tell. It had been the most momentous eighteen months of my life. You could condense it down; the last year of my life, the last six months of my life, was huge. It was – when Grant and I started the Go-Betweens, we were boys. And now I was – I'd recorded the album; I was there on my thirty-third birthday. It was a new chapter in so many ways. And so, there was much ground to cover. So much had happened with the break-up of the band, with me finding – I was married, you know; we married in May. There was – so much had happened to my life over the previous eighteen months. For that song cycle, to bring that down to five songs, that wasn't enough time.

PC: This album really works as a song cycle, something you could achieve only with the space you were given.

RF: Only. I could only have done it that way. And even if Grant and I had done a double album at that time, it still would have been mixed up in his story. So, look, and I was conscious of that when I was writing, you know for the first time, I didn't just go, you know, 'Five'. When I was in the Go-Betweens, I could write five fairly disconnected songs, because Grant would have his five, and somehow that would weld into something real. Whereas this was like, I've gotta cover the whole thing and this gives me opportunities I've never had before.

PC: The album also struck me as being like a series of linked short stories or filmic vignettes.

RF: I like those kinds of songs, and I hadn't really written them before. But I never saw myself at that time as a frustrated filmmaker or frustrated short-story writer at that particular moment. I was still very much – I saw myself strictly as a singer-songwriter. But I was always interested in broadening what I did. I'd always liked stories from '70s songs. Any time when I was a young person I heard on the radio someone telling a story, I somehow found it fascinating. But I didn't want to – the obvious way that that is done was in folk music, which the Irish are masters of, but I wasn't that kind of, I wasn't from that tradition, I wasn't from that folk tradition. So, I had to sort of work my way into it and just put it into my songs. Which I did. And which you know with something like 'Danger in the Past' and 'I've Been Looking for Somebody', I started to really find a language in the music to do that. You know, at that moment.

PC: When the album came out, did you have a sense of achievement?

RF: Yeah. It was what I wanted it to be. Without wishing to – this is going to sound enormously egotistical – I wanted it to be a classic record. I was listening to – there were a couple of first albums that stayed in my mind. John Lennon's first solo album. John Phillips, who was the singer and songwriter of the Mamas and the Papas, made a solo album called *Wolf King of L.A.*, which I had as well, which was an amazing record. He wrote a 400-page book, and the album got half a page. So, I don't know what he ever thought of it. But I wanted to make something like that, something like *Plastic Ono Band*. Something like John Prine's first album.

PC: You were setting the bar pretty high. Was there a reason you went in with the intention of making a classic?

RF: The Go-Betweens' first album is not a classic. And I just wanted to make – I was hoping to . . . You can go into a record honestly and you have the material, and you don't make that record. I always find, going into a studio with something, I can guess about 60 per cent of it. It just happens in the studio. No matter how much you prepare, how slowly you work, you think you're going in to make something, and you come out with something that's slightly different or totally different.

PC: This time it worked out.

RF: It did, it did. The fact is that all the decisions were right. Mick Harvey was right. Hansa was right. Victor was right. The musicians were right. The songs met the sound. I'd written the songs. And I knew it really caught that moment in my life, that big moment in my life. So, I was very, very happy with that record. And so, to me, I didn't even want to tour it. I was so tired. I was so wrecked from the Go-Betweens, I didn't want to tour. First time ever, you know, that's how burnt-out I was from touring. It was a record I was really just happy to sit in a house and let it go out into the world and just know I'd done it.

PC: It occurred to me that the three words Karin sang on the title song ('Danger' repeated twice) are like a stamp or a watermark on the album to seal the beginning of your new life. The future was going to be different.

RF: I can see that the material I was writing, although I wouldn't have been able to articulate it in that moment, was not fit for the Go-Betweens. I was writing material inspired by the music I was listening to – I was listening to singer-songwriters, I've said this before, like Guy Clark and Townes Van Zandt. I was listening to country music. I was listening to folk music. There was a natural style for me that I developed into. I knew I didn't want to compete with the Pixies or Dinosaur Jr. Or what was coming out of Manchester, the Happy Mondays. I knew I had nothing to do with that anymore.

PC: The music was leading you somewhere else now.

RF: This new music had come in and it's all bound up. It's not like I'd completely changed. The songs that I wrote on *16 Lovers Lane*, like 'Clouds', 'I'm All Right', 'Love Is a Sign', 'Dive for Your Memory' – it's all in this as well. It's a natural thing but it's just twisted and changed. It's deeper. People ask me, you know, why did the Go-Betweens break up? I almost feel like handing them *Danger in the Past* and going, 'well, you listen to *that*'. It's still a record where I think that's one thing I see in hindsight. The other thing is how well it catches that moment. And it was one of those three or four times in your life where things change in a profound way, where your art struggles to catch up to how much is going on. So, I see that. And I'm just really proud of the sound of it. I don't think it's dated. I think it's got that room in Berlin. I'm very proud of it. Very, very proud of that record.

***

Happy to have made an album as good as any by the Go-Betweens, Robert was also glad to learn that Edwyn Collins liked *Danger in the Past*. However, he declined an opportunity to go on the road with his old Postcard friend. Exhaustion was one reason, and an unwillingness to leave Karin again after they had just married.

For Robert, it had been quite a journey since that night in Munich when Bill Berry's illness had finally brought him and Karin together; that first time she had put on his red dress and found that it fit them both perfectly.

7 The songs

'Baby Stones'

Music is time travel. Listen to two songs recorded decades apart by the same singer and you cross the years instantly. Soon after I first heard 'Karen', I heard 'Baby Stones'. I adored 'Karen' as a love song to a librarian who helps the singer find Hemingway, Genet, Brecht, Chandler, James Joyce. Clinton Walker says it's about his sister Lisa, who worked in a bookshop, but Robert insists it's not.[1] This paean to a bookish muse written as if she were a dominatrix (and why not?) is a young man's song. Between 'I just want some affection', the opening line of 'Karen', and 'You say you want to take a lover / although you're satisfied with us', which kicks off 'Baby Stones', there is an ocean of living. From the raw, impulsive energy of the former to the veiled tenderness of the latter, the singer, unlike the time-travelling listener, must take the long way around.

'Baby Stones' is the more sophisticated and subtle piece. It's not trying to have a concept, although it does have one. The narrator has been hurt and tries to hide it, his casual equanimity a façade. 'So go and see him; what will be, will be.' That line in the chorus sounds like Zen detachment until it is swiftly undermined as he hits us with: 'Every man for the rest of your life will be less than me.' A note of pathos, if not an expression of weakness; it's also wryly funny until the pleading begins. 'I want you to stay.' This is more than the self-abasement of a soon-to-be-forsaken lover. It implies blame for destroying something beautiful. 'You search for a worthwhile need. / But why not do the searching around here / and try and involve me?' Like that's going to work. For redemption to occur, there has to be something to redeem. 'Baby Stones' is about acceptance. It avoids the misogyny so common in rock. This is not, say, The Beatles' 'Run for Your Life' with its threat of murder, control and violent abuse.[2] In 'Baby Stones', the narrator is just a man standing in front of a woman, daring her to go, and he's being quite catty about it. The singer addresses his subject directly, 'you' rather than 'she'. It's a conversation, not a report; not a male singer bragging or moaning to an audience of men about the woman in his life, which often comes across as possessive, even consumerist: 'Uptown Girl' by Billy Joel is a good example. 'Baby Stones' gets nicely passive-aggressive too, which adds to the fun. 'So excuse me if I look tired. / Excuse me if I just look at the sun. / You see I wanted to be blinded / and I wanted to be your only one.' That longing is familiar to anyone who has lost in love and been on either side of an apparently simple question for which there is no simple answer: 'What was wrong with us?' Intentionally or otherwise, the lyric echoes the great jazz-blues standard 'I'd Rather Go Blind', recorded by Etta James in 1967.

Regret is the superpower of the pop lyricist, and it's often most eloquently deployed, as here, in the contrast between a bright, open sound and dry, melancholy lyrics. Released as a single before the album itself, 'Baby Stones' seems too idiosyncratic to have been a hit in 1990. This is not 'Another Day in Paradise' or 'Pump Up the Jam'. It's not even 'Nothing Compares 2U'.

As in many sincere songs, the narrative 'I' is not the writer. In *Grant & I*, Robert relates how the lyric was inspired by a situation he observed during an early stay at Karin's house in Alteglofsheim.

> My songwriting recommenced. I'd written a melody and was in need of a lyric when a friend of Karin's visited with boyfriend problems, there being two of them. Subject matter found, I placed myself as the aggrieved partner addressing his girlfriend.[3]

Its lyrical perspective makes 'Baby Stones' something of a companion, almost an answer song, to 'Rock'n'Roll Friend'.

PC: Do you think such fictional narratives inevitably express something personal anyway?

RF: Yes, I do. Although I wasn't the person in the three-way relationship the song describes, all the angles and imagined emotions I insert in the song spring from a well or a place inside of me. Another writer would write the song in a completely different way. Also, 'Baby Stones', with all its talk of break-ups and tensions and new beginnings, which I wrote in Bavaria in November '89, for the band to break up in Sydney in December – I found at the time a little spooky. If something was in the air, I'd touched it, or perhaps it was just coincidence.

With 'Baby Stones', the album begins as it means to go on. It's a Dylanesque opening statement, a poised declaration of intent, and you can almost dance to it.

'The River People'

Inspired by a fantastical source, Rupert Bunny's oil painting *Tritons*, 'The River People' has a cinematic atmosphere and makes me think of *The Last Wave* by Peter Weir (Figure 7.1).[4] The lyrics place imagery from the painting alongside scenes that portray the workings of small-town prejudice at a meeting where outsiders are met with hostility. 'Down here / everybody says that the River People don't really belong there', leads on to 'Your stranded face before moonlight / the colour of the sea / You came / up to the house after swimming on sunset and the flattened sea'.

> **PC:** Was there a real-world story that you blended with the mythic in this song?
>
> **RF:** No, not really. The story came from feelings or impressions I got off the people in the painting. They looked like outsiders. Sea creatures. Late-nineteenth-century hippies.

Figure 7.1 *Rupert Bunny (Australia/France 1864–1947)*, Tritons *c.1890, oil on canvas, 80.3 × 150.5 cm. Art Gallery of New South Wales, purchased 1969, Image © Art Gallery of New South Wales*

And perhaps there is a little feeling of me being the outsider who had come to this small little Bavarian town, living in the farmhouse – that got shuffled in there too. But there is no real-world story to the song. It was coming off the painting. I remember, I stood before it in a Sydney gallery, writing poetic notes in a diary and then wrote the melody later and they fit.

Robert spoke about *Tritons* and played 'The River People' at the Art Gallery of New South Wales for the exhibition *Photography & Place: Australian Landscape Photography, 1970s Until Now*, on 13 April 2011, where he elaborated on the song's inspiration.[5] In early 1988, when the Go-Betweens returned to Sydney to make *16 Lovers Lane*, he moved into a terraced house at Broughton Street in Woolloomooloo. He used to walk to the gallery, which was nearby and spend time with the paintings. The nineteenth-century art there nourished him the most – especially the work of the Symbolist painter Sydney Long.

After making the album, the band toured for the next year and came back to the city, exhausted from the road, towards the end of 1989. Robert moved into a flat in Bondi Junction, having begun his relationship with Karin during the tour. Wanting to be with her rather than here, he found refuge in the gallery, with a feeling that although the art hadn't changed, he had, no longer as joyous as when he'd first discovered it. For solace, he came back to the same paintings he'd visited before. Now, one touched him above the others: *Tritons*. He described it for his audience,

It was a seascape done just at the end of the day and there's people in the water and there's one man who's looking directly at the viewer and he's got long hair and a beard and although this painting was done in 1890 he looks like a full-on hippie.[6]

During these visits to the gallery, Robert would also view the work of Sydney Nolan (1917–1992), Brett Whiteley[7] (1939–1992), Russell Drysdale (1912–1981), and others. None of these artists affected him in the same way that Bunny did.

Rupert Bunny, born in Melbourne in 1864, was thirty-six when he painted *Tritons* in 1890, almost a hundred years before Robert first saw it. Celebrated in France, some of his work hangs in the Musée du Luxembourg, but this painting remains in Australia. *Tritons* depicts the titular mythical figures relaxing at evening in a state of tranquillity between the land and the sea. On Sunday afternoons, Robert used to sit before the picture and find himself absorbed in it. One day, after his return to Alteglofsheim in 1990, he was composing songs in the farmhouse and found a chord progression and a melody that spoke to him. For lyrics, he went to his notebook and, between working on the music and his impressions of *Tritons*, he added new lyrical elements, all of which combined to become 'The River People'. It sounds like a folk song, the vocal unusually plaintive, the music austere and crystalline. In 1991, on his next visit to Australia to play a concert and see friends, Robert took Karin to the gallery to share with her the painting that had led to the song.

'The River People', in turn, inspired the Walkabouts, a Seattle band, to cover it in 1993.[8] Would Robert be interested in having someone put together an *I'm Your Fan*-style covers album of his solo work?

RF: Their version is great, taken at a faster clip. An *I'm Your Fan* album[9] of my solo work would be lovely.

'Leave Here Satisfied'

'Where are you now, where are you now. Where are you now my friend.'

Bruce Robinson's 1986 film *Withnail & I*[10] centres on the exploits of a pair of actors adrift at the end of the sixties. It also serves as a stinging satire on Thatcher's Britain. In the story, one character commits to a dissolute life while his friend leaves it all behind to pursue a theatre career in the 'straight' world. A choice is made, paths diverge and nothing will ever be the same. It's easy to imagine the Go-Betweens and their fellows in London living in the kind of shabby-genteel squalor that marked the house in that film, a dissolute lifestyle that eventually forces you to sink into it or leave. It's easy also to think of Grant and Robert coming to a similar crucial nexus in their relationship at the break-up of their band. Is it possible that the title of Robert's memoir *Grant & I* alludes to Robinson's film?

Danger in the Past becomes ever more confessional in 'Leave Here Satisfied', and the sense of loss at its heart lends credence to the idea that this album is Robert Forster's *Blood on the Tracks*. Not a conventional love song by any means, 'Leave Here Satisfied' is a plea to Grant. Its love is fraternal, injured, an intervention perhaps, opening a hand that the other may take, yet knowing it might be a while before the offer is accepted.

RF: In the immediate aftermath of the Go-Betweens' break-up in Sydney in late December 1989, Grant was living in a house down the road from an apartment he had been living in, that I had taken over. Each day I would go down to his house to see him. Knock on the front door – no answer. Peer in windows. Wait. And finally, he would shuffle to the front door and open it. I never knew what I'd find. He was in a very bad way. I wrote a melody a few months later in Bavaria that I knew was big and needed something big as a lyric, and I thought of these creeping visits.

The song's placement in the running order reveals the arc of the album's overall narrative. This is a farewell to Sydney as well as to Grant. Side One is full of doubt, felt most keenly here, in a song with a pair of living ghosts at its heart, haunting each other. The one (Grant) who may or may not be in, or even alive; the other (Robert) compelled to show up every day, to make sure that his friend is still there, still with us. That might be all there is to say about the inspiration for 'Leave Here Satisfied', a song whose resonance is as troubling as it is powerful.

Possibly the saddest lyric on *Danger in the Past*, it is a tale of two soulmates knowing they must separate as one moves away to a new life. But the narrator can't abandon his best friend. Robert can't go without knowing that Grant will survive.

Here is a telling line: 'There was dust on the piano keys, dust on the backyard trees, dust on the door locks but not on me.' In the midst of his concern, their relationship newly full of heart-in-mouth uncertainty, the narrator recognizes his own purpose, and the need to avoid the drowning man's grip.

Another telling line: 'I could go but I wouldn't leave here satisfied.' If he hadn't found his anchor in love, would Robert have had the strength to help his friend and not lose himself? It doesn't make the song's dilemma any less painful, but I think so.

Mick Harvey's arrangement holds Robert's voice like a setting holds a jewel. It moves between intimate verses as he speaks directly to the listener and a bounding chorus that feels like a poltergeist whirlwind, shaking the emotional furniture of the narrator's mind. You can really hear the space of that enormous room at Hansa and how every cubic inch of it was needed.

'Heart Out to Tender'

A song that knows the value of longing, of waiting, 'Heart Out to Tender' looks to the future but leaves a wistful note behind for the life the narrator has to forgo in order to claim his new romance. And that seems to be the right phrase: to claim. He has to step up, to prove himself worthy. A love song to Karin, 'Heart Out to Tender' also works without the listener having to know the inspiration for its characters. In *Grant & I*, Robert recalls the courtly progress of his and Karin's correspondence by letter and phone while he was out on the road.[11] That chimes with the way this song tells its story. 'I came along with my bid', he sings. A petition rather than a demand. The playfulness of 'Baby Stones' is not so much to be found here: 'She gets bigger in the mirror / I have to be with her this time.' Does that couplet speak of inevitability or hope? It's not the narrator's heart that's out to tender, but his vulnerability is clear, and there's no rock-star posturing. Love is to be won, but the singer's bid collateral must surely be no less than his own heart.

After a Hepatitis C diagnosis at the age of thirty-nine in 1997,[12] Robert gave up being intoxicated by anything but beauty, whereas Grant continued to consume that which would consume him. It was another way in which their paths in life diverged. 'Heart Out to Tender' may be read as a premonitory prayer of acceptance and a recognition that a new way forward was required. Musically, it is loose and dreamlike; a train song, too, with its rhythm calling back to early rock and roll. Robert says it was a new kind of song for him.

> **RF:** More rootsy. A country twang. A different, more straight-ahead language to the lyric. I wrote it immediately after the Go-Betweens broke up, so I don't know how the band would have handled it. I don't mean this in any kind of judgmental way in regard to the Go-Betweens' musical skills – but I don't know how many of the songs on *Danger in the Past* the band could have played. Many of the songs are outside of what I'd written before. It was like I went into a different mode. Some of them needed little or no drums for example.

'Heart Out to Tender' uses very light percussion, a shuffle, perfectly arranged for what the song requires. Which is not to say that Lindy couldn't have done it – she surely could have – but this was a different set-up altogether.

If this album might be considered Robert's *Plastic Ono Band*, 'Heart Out to Tender' is one of the songs in favour of that idea, although Lennon's songs to Yoko Ono are all too apologetic to be romantic. Here, the singer is not in the business of abasing himself.

Coming to it new, the listener may find uncertainty in the verses. Knowing that the bid was accepted turns the song into a celebration of self-confidence; a quiet one, all the same, in keeping with the restraint that gives the album strength. 'Heart Out to Tender' is an effective prelude to the starker, bleaker song that follows it.

'Is This What You Call Change'

If this lyric had been written about you, you'd have questions. If this were Dylan, it'd be 'Positively 4th Street'.[13] It's a dark ending to Side One and marks a clear division in the record. After this, acceptance enters the picture and hope begins to flow. But first, there's an uncompromising calling to account of . . . someone. It could be Bjelke-Petersen. 'As I breathe your deadly wind / As the oil in the river sends / Everything that's alive / To a painful end'. It surely can't be about any of Robert's bandmates, or his seven-year relationship with Lindy Morrison. It might be simply a lyric that emerged, as they do, and the writer let it flow. Goodness knows there was plenty going wrong in the world at the time for it to be a political song, yet it could be about drugs. With shades of 'How Do You Sleep?'[14] is it about betrayal? 'You stuck a knife in our side. Is this what you call change?' The song is crestfallen enough to be about humanity itself. It is also rinsed in regret. After the title song, this is the strongest lyric on the album.

PC: Was there a particular influence on the creation of 'Is This What You Call Change'?

RF: As I remember, this was the first song I wrote after *16 Lovers Lane*. I am not counting 'Rock'n'Roll Friend', as I started writing that when we were making *16 Lovers Lane*. The song struck me as something different and new when I wrote it – not at all a rock song. It mystified me, although I liked it a great deal. It was downbeat. Not a springing rock number bouncing you into a new round of songwriting for a coming album.

This is a perfectly reasonable response. As any writer will tell you, we don't always know where our inspiration comes from at any given moment. All we can do is to be in the place where the work happens, and invite it in. And sometimes what comes is a song like this.

The arrangement is reminiscent of the direction in which the Bad Seeds had just gone with *The Good Son*, and you could imagine Nick Cave doing a brooding cover of 'Is This What You Call Change'. Yet it's the fragility of Robert's own voice that injects a sense of sorrow beneath the accusation in the lyric. A colder tone will infuse 'On a Street Corner' on his 1996 album *Warm Nights* but that side to his writing starts to flow here. Surprisingly brief after the four longer songs that precede it, 'Is This What You Call Change' doesn't hang around too long. Maybe it's too painful for the song itself to persist.

It is hard to think of Grant playing on 'Is This What You Call Change'. His sunnier music often clothes bitter lyrics but even he never got so stark. With this song, Robert really had entered new territory, a future as an artist that he was possibly unaware had already begun.

'Dear Black Dream'

This is almost country music, but it doesn't feature some trucker losing his marriage, his job, his mind and his liver. Or his dog. A celebration of comfort and domestic stability, 'Dear Black Dream' portrays the narrator waking after a dark dream of a strange hotel. His lover soothes him, and the song ends with them sitting in bed, wondering who sings better in the dark: Townes Van Zandt or Guy Clark. The kind of conversation Robert might once have had with Grant and probably did, he is now having with his wife. The hotel here prefigures the idea of the past as a place, which the following song expresses so brilliantly.

Robert's interest in writing in a purely singer-songwriter style flourished in Bavaria, where Karin and her bandmates in Baby You Know were fans of Clark, Townes, Dylan and Johnny Cash. He reflects:

> In a beautiful coincidence, Guy Clark and Townes Van Zandt were followed here too, and, in true German style, were followed in depth: a bootleg video of the seventies Texan-outlaw, country-scene documentary *Heartworn Highways*, with eye-popping footage of Guy and Townes and a sixteen-year-old Steve Earle, was a key inspiration.[15]

A couple of years earlier, before an acoustic Go-Betweens show at McCabe's in Santa Monica, Guy Clark came into their dressing room to see who was playing, as he and Townes were to perform there the following night.

> The next evening, watching Clark on stage, two songs in, I knew I was in the presence of a master singer-songwriter, the best I'd seen up close.[16]

In June 2008, Robert discussed his appreciation for Guy Clark with *Mojo* magazine:

> He's a master. I started to listen to him a lot in the late '80s and he taught me economy. There's a great dignity to his songwriting. He put out his first album, *Old No. 1*, in 1975, in his mid-thirties, which I thought was fantastic: this is from a grown man, who's done a bit, seen a bit, and managed to get it down.

The seventh track on Clark's *Old No. 1*, 'Desperados Waiting For A Train', was a radio favourite in Ireland in the 1978 live version by Freddie White, which is how I first heard it. It is easy to imagine Robert covering that song in his new, folkier style.

PC: At a certain point, did you align yourself with these classic American singer-songwriters?

RF: I did. I liked their combination of strong melody and stellar lyric writing. A combination to songwriting I always loved, but Guy and Townes brought a new twist. And they seemed grown up, and they'd lived and seen things and got it down in song. I was thirty and going into my early thirties, and it was the music I wanted to hear, and it influenced me, no doubt.

'Danger in the Past'

One of the best songs in Robert Forster's catalogue, this is a clear-eyed recollection of difficult times. Its remembrance of lost people and places prefigures such story-songs as 'Darlinghurst Nights' on *Oceans Apart* but 'Danger in the Past' is more dreamlike, more brittle. It would have been a remarkable entry in the Go-Betweens canon if they had stayed together, but as often mentioned, it would not have been an entry in the Go-Betweens canon at all. The theme of a writer returning to a place only to find that he's 'made enemies while I was away' reminds us that we can't step into the same river twice. It's a common idea in fiction and folk music, but what counts here is how it's done. Poetry is the key to this song, or at least to one of its many rooms. The Confessional poets were among its midwives as much as were the folk-country singer-songwriters Robert was listening to at the time: Anne Sexton and Sylvia Plath are two of the references that Robert cites; I also detect a tincture of Robert Lowell.[17] Sexton's '45 Mercy Street' comes to mind, a poem that Peter Gabriel used as a source four years earlier on his smash-hit 1986 album, *So*. The song, simply called 'Mercy Street', is devastating, one of Gabriel's best.[18]

'Danger in the Past' was an important song to me as a young poet, and it retains its power to inspire, conjuring a specific time and place to tell a universal story of how we must grow if we are to survive. Loss and grief, resilience and love, regret and compassion – all find expression in the song's musical arrangement, which is simultaneously stately and propulsive, its confident momentum carrying a lyric both widescreen and intimate.

Mental illness, the AIDS epidemic, the loss of young people to suicide, all flow as shadow subjects within its streams of meaning. On the surface, 'Danger in the Past' is about visiting someone in hospital, but it goes deeper. Here are the lyrics, the refrain's repetition simplified for the page.

Danger in the Past

Your sister picked me up at the station
She told me they'd taken you in
The word was it was just observation
I thought here we go again

Danger in the Past

So I went and I saw you
We walked through the hospital grounds
I took your hand and I told you
Never show your problems in a country town

Danger in the Past

We had friends
We had friends that didn't make twenty-five
I knew a genius in a bedroom who couldn't walk outside
There have been some tremors in our lives

Danger in the Past

Your mother is a saint
With her goodwill and with strength
I think that she thought that we were once lovers
Now she seems happier that we're friends

Danger in the Past

That refrain, a simple restatement of the title in between the verses, acts like a scene transition. As Pete Paphides has suggested, the phrase contains several potential readings. There's danger in looking back at the past. Or the danger is in the past. We may take it as either a warning or a sigh of relief. It may even strike a note of nostalgia for troubled times: the pain of remembrance. Nostalgia, according to its original definition, is a severe and sometimes fatal form of melancholia due to homesickness.[19]

'Danger in the Past' alone makes its parent album different, a true departure from what had gone before, one of those key points in a writer's work after which everything is new. Robert told *Uncut* that when you write a song like this, it 'changes your perception of who you are as a songwriter'.[20]

PC: What's your relationship with 'Danger in the Past' now?

RF: I've always been somewhat in awe of it. Unlike anything I had written before. I have said this in the past – it's like a good Guy Clark or Dylan folk verse, folk melody, with a lyric soaked in the Anne Sexton and Sylvia Plath poetry I had been gorging myself on over the previous years. It was that unexpected combination. Two trains running through me in those years that really intersected in this song. When I hit, 'we walked through the hospital grounds', I knew I was onto something.

'Danger in the Past' is one of those Proustian memory songs that have shown up in Robert's canon – and they haven't all been this dark. 'German Farmhouse', 'Surfing Magazines' and 'Darlinghurst Nights' are surely lighter. For other songs with the emotional gravity of 'Danger in the Past', listen to two of his later albums. The first is *The Evangelist*. Recorded after the death of Grant, it features the elegiac 'Demon Days' and 'From Ghost Town'. Its title track addresses how Robert brought Karin from her world into his, and the adjustment that entailed. The second album to consider is *The Candle and the Flame*, most of it written before Karin's cancer diagnosis in 2021[21] but recorded afterwards, while the family rallied around her, during the ongoing COVID-19 pandemic. The theme of danger in the work of Robert Forster – sometimes appearing from out of the past, sometimes freshly sprung in the now – has given rise to magnificent songs. And for all that in concert he performs it with a certain flamboyance, 'Danger in the Past' remains one of Robert's most mysteriously moving compositions.

'I've Been Looking for Somebody' and 'Justice'

'I've Been Looking for Somebody' and 'Justice' form a pair. These two songs are where the album declares for hope. The former is the second song in a row that refers to coming back to 'my own city', but this visit is different. Dawn approaches though the lingering traces of the previous night. This is the end of the Go-Betweens, the end of wilder times. In real life, all of that had to finish before the resolution, and there's relief, even, at the prospect: 'the party's over, that's when she came.' The implication that if the party hadn't ended, she might not have come, recalls the dilemma of 'Heart Out to Tender'. Here it is resolved. The danger is in the past, and the future is all about being fully alive.

'When I was younger, foolish and naïve / I used to think there was no woman in this world for me / But now I've changed, I've changed my mind.' Finally settled on his new course, the narrator contrasts his former self with the happier person he's become, having found what – and who – he was searching for. With 'And then she came', the story that the album tells reaches a satisfying resolution.

> **RF:** It does. And something in me at the time must have known that, and so I sequenced this after 'Danger in the Past'; and 'Justice' fitted perfectly after it. Just thinking of these songs now, I cannot imagine them fitting into the Go-Betweens' sound or working methods. And yet I wrote them before the band broke up, thinking they would be on the group's next album.

Musically as well as lyrically, the climactic dance into the light of 'I've Been Looking for Somebody' leads directly to the denouement of 'Justice', a gently propulsive song that leaves us with a sense of direction as well as hope. The album rests its case, and the narrator, after songs of doubt and fear, love and grief, yearning and acceptance, has achieved the momentum he needed in order to grow into himself. In 'I've Been Looking for Somebody', he uses the words 'I love you' for the first time but has someone else say them: a 'passing angel' who wants a smoke. In 'Justice', he describes what that 'I love you' feels like. 'There's lace at the door / And a fire upstairs / There's smoke in the night / And someone who cares.' That fire is not the one that cannot 'burn on the same old wood' mentioned in 'Baby Stones'. It's the hearth of his new home.

PC: The song seems to be about gratitude. Did the title, 'Justice' carry any particular meaning for you at that point in your life and career?

RF: It was the gratitude that Karin and I had finally gotten together through all the waiting and postponing and wrong timing of the previous years. What we were feeling was right and it had been rewarded, and here we were living together in the one house. I have to very much thank Mick Harvey for this song being on the album. We were a song short in Hansa Studios in Berlin, and I played it to him, not knowing what he'd make of it. He was enthusiastic, immediately digging out an old Bakelite organ from the 1950s – these sorts of instruments were covered in dust in cupboards in Hansa – and we began recording.

Doing Things Differently

8 The anchor

Robert writes in *Grant & I* of the anchor we carry around – one that centres us in our lives. It can also tether us to chaos. This idea made me think not only of the situation he was moving into during the making of *Danger in the Past* but also of the French novelist Gustave Flaubert's exhortation: 'Soyez réglé dans votre vie et ordinaire comme un bourgeois, afin d'être violent et original dans vos oeuvres.' This comes from a letter to Gertrude Tennant, dated 25 December 1876. 'Be regular and orderly in your life like a bourgeois, so that you may be violent and original in your work', is a close translation in English, the one we are most familiar with, although there is a subtly different meaning to be found in the original: be regular in your life and *ordinary* like a bourgeois.

Flaubert's advice is the opposite of literary critic Cyril Connolly's 'There is no more sombre enemy of good art than the pram in the hall.'[1] The idea of the artist who sacrifices everything else in the pursuit of art is romantic, but ultimately such a lifestyle is unsustainable without requiring the sacrifice, or at least the support, of others. As the ambient-music pioneer Brian Eno argues in his idea of the 'scenius',[2] there are no solitary geniuses at work without at least the tacit consent of others. An anchoress needs a village to supply her solitude; an artist depends on those who work in a paper mill or a quarry or a forge or a brewery.

Author J. G. Ballard, disagreeing with Connolly, raised three children after the death of his wife Mary, and managed to be prodigious and brilliant, although Ballard did suggest that it was his children who brought *him* up.[3] Yet, Virginia Woolf's statement, 'A woman must have money and a room of her own if she is to write fiction' is still relevant today.[4] All kinds of impediments can make it difficult, if not impossible, to pursue the art life. The means of production is what it boils down to. Making art requires space, time and focus; it needs dedication and the permission to apply it. For some people, it is possible to create great work but at the cost of their own mental and physical health. Is that sacrifice worth it, or can it even be avoided? It depends on who is asking. For others, the work improves when they find some kind of personal equilibrium. The late, great filmmaker and artist David Lynch reminded us in his book *Catching the Big Fish* that an artist needs a 'setup'.[5] How that is achieved, and what comes out of it, depends on the artist and their circumstances. It might be an expansive recording suite in West Berlin or an hour's break grabbed daily in order to write. Dissolution is not always required, nor is even a mild stimulant. *Ambit* magazine ran a competition in 1968 for the best work written while taking drugs; it was won by the novelist Ann Quin, who had written her piece, *Tripticks*, under the influence of the contraceptive pill, Orthonovin 2.[6]

When I ask Robert what he makes of Flaubert's advice, his first reaction is simply, 'Wow'.

PC: Does that resonate with you?
RF: It does. It does. I think. That's interesting. Orderly in your life so you can be disorderly or violent in your work. I

think that's totally true. And I think that's something that I've always had – and people talk about it – I come from a happy childhood, and I think I've got better as I've got older as an orderly person. I'm not a particularly tidy person, but I think my house is in order spiritually, which allows me to go, with some confidence, where I wanted to go to.

PC: Clearly, that wasn't also true of Grant.

RF: It's something that Grant didn't have. Grant floated. Grant was the most untethered person I ever met. He didn't have that foundation. And he – I think in his work he could go where he – I could hear it in his work. He's a person at times in despair, and it's quite naked. And it's almost like with Grant – and this used to frustrate me a little bit – he's always talking in poetic language. There's a sort of self-conscious poeticism to Grant. And I think it's in part because he hasn't got that order that you talk about, to write about. So, everything's – you have to read between the lines with him to get actually where he is. There's very few of his songs where he's addressing you directly. It's always a little bit – it's always a little bit hazy with a lot of poetics, you know. And I think this is that he could at times – he found difficulty telling it straight because his life was not happy for periods. I don't want to talk about in circles here. He was a very complicated person. Very, very complicated.

I recognize this in Robert's descriptions of Grant in his book. It isn't necessarily the best way to live if you want to survive. And, as noted above, for some artists it isn't always required. David Bowie, late in life, used to keep regular hours in the studio, having in his younger years pushed himself and his musicians to breaking point.

Still, I understand the drive to give absolutely everything to the work, even as it alienates others, even as it isolates the artist. The making of art is not a passive experience, not just something that simply happens to an artist, all other things being equal. It's a choice that comes at a cost. Even the most cerebral art requires physical and emotional expenditure, and how that is managed depends on the individual. Creative self-destructiveness can be confounding to those who live around the artist. Robert alludes to this in 'Rock'n'Roll Friend', which takes the perspective of a girlfriend addressing the narrator who comes home from the road, smelling of the music that he makes.

PC: Grant, with no hesitation, appears to have gone all in on the art life.

RF: Yeah, you're exactly right. This was a problem. That he, in a strange way, and it's with these people, you might know it – you can come to the conclusion that this is what they want, as well, which is frightening to me. But that's what they want. There are also people, and Grant was one of them, who have a very, very intense relationship with art because it's something to hold on to. It gives a meaning to life more than if you, going back to this Flaubert thing – an orderly life – you've got some sort of stability, though you love art. But for people that are – and this is probably an extreme, talking about Grant – damaged, he was the most romantic person in regard to art. He saw existence, he saw sustenance in art, which in a way he struggled to find that in life, so he saw it in art. So, there's books everywhere, there's poetry books everywhere, there's films everywhere, and he loses himself in that and is happy to lose himself in that because it's a place to go to.

PC: This is one of the reasons I asked the Flaubert question, because it seems to me now, perhaps counterintuitively, when you let people in, your work can improve. It can mature.

RF: Yeah, yeah, I think so. I agree. And I was very lucky at this time. This was my great luck to have met Karin at that time, at that period when the Go-Betweens were ending, although we'd known each other for a couple of years before we got together. That was my great fortune. Because although she was younger than me, she was an extremely stable person, and I recognized that. And besides all her other qualities, I knew that I was not with a wild person, I was with someone who was very anchor-like. I was very lucky with that. She was a consistent person. That's something she says of me, that I was a consistent person. I always kept to promises I made, and she always kept to promises that she made, and I think that was probably the great link between us.

PC: And Bob Dylan.

RF: And Bob Dylan. Yeah, well, you know, God, if you meet a beautiful woman who loves Bob Dylan, it's the jackpot.

9 *Freakchild* variations

Beatles fans have been doing it for decades – compellingly in the case of Charles Hazlewood's 2017 documentary for Sky Arts, *My Beatles Black Album* – seeing if a windfall band LP could be made out of the members' first solo records.[1] After *Watershed* and *Danger in the Past* came out, Go-Betweens fans followed suit, making mixtapes that combined tracks from the two singers' debuts, attempting to create a 'new' Go-Betweens record.

As we know, some of the songs on *Danger in the Past* had been intended for *Freakchild*. What could they have sounded like as fully worked up Go-Betweens tunes? Quite different, we must imagine, given the personnel and recording methods that would have been used, either for a full-band album or the proposed duo project. The demos show how the music was already highly worked out, with only a few lyrical variations from the eventual recordings, notably on 'I've Been Looking for Somebody'.[2] Do the circumstances of their birth give these songs a special kind of intensity? Are *Danger in the Past* or *Watershed* equivalent to Lennon's *Plastic Ono Band* or McCartney's *Ram*? I asked Robert if he understood this phenomenon.

> **RF:** No, I don't. As I said, there was a record we *could* have made. I must say, and this is one of the highest things I can say about *Danger in the Past*, I'm so glad that we never made

that record. Because *Danger in the Past* means so much to me. And I think it's of a quality that I would not want it *not* to have been made. And so, I can talk jokingly about, you know, in a fantasy about an album we would have made but I'm glad that we didn't make it. Grant had a lot of songs. I had about nine things to pick from when we would have made that record and if we had gone in that direction that we were talking about of making a non-commercial folk record to be the seventh Go-Betweens record – artistically we were ready to do it and we were ready after making the pop gem *16 Lovers Lane*, which again was a true record but it didn't give us the pot of gold. We were ready to make any kind of record. We were open to spitting in the face of the whole system, not to piss them off but 'we're going to make a downbeat folk record'.

PC: There's a passion in that.

RF: Yeah, and we would have done – Grant would have been up to it, I think. Honestly, he saw that record, *16 Lovers Lane*, which was easily the most commercial record we'd ever made, and he was a very commercial person; he saw it hadn't worked, and I think although he was always a melody person and a production person, I think he would have gone down the route of 'let's just make the record we wanna make'. And we wouldn't have made it with Mark Wallis [producer of *16 Lovers Lane*]. It would have been – I don't know how we would have done it.

Various permutations of a mooted *Freakchild* have surfaced over the years, all including tracks that appeared on neither solo album. In 2002, the Go-Betweens' label Circus Records compiled a version using live recordings from the original band's last show in Sydney in 1989 and demos from the Botany sessions. This was never issued and remains another 'what-if' mixtape.[3]

In any case, the next album would not have been a full-band Go-Betweens record, as Robert has observed. These new songs may have grown differently in the context of the band, but given the creative directions the two songwriters pursued, their styles would have clashed like never before. The difference between *Watershed*'s pop polish and *Danger in the Past*'s more organic sound indicates that Grant's record and Robert's needed to be made separately. For what it's worth, you could interleave the two and make a double, but the only double that even remotely works for *Danger in the Past* is to present it as the first half of a set with Robert's second solo album, *Calling from a Country Phone*.

Grant's music had changed, too. Not all of his new songs were potential Go-Betweens tracks. He'd already broken away from his partnership with Robert thanks to 'Streets of Your Town'. Now, with Jack Frost on the go as well as his solo record in the offing, the distance grew ever greater. When the Go-Betweens reformed with *The Friends of Rachel Worth*, it felt like two complementary solo artists sharing space, and it wasn't until *Oceans Apart* that they found it again fully – their old communion.

Painful as their separation was, the so-called intermission needed to happen. Robert seems to agree, because the record he actually made, rather than those that often played in our imaginings, was the best possible outcome for these songs. As Yogi Berra put it, 'when you come to a fork in the road, take it'.[4] G. W. McLennan and Robert Forster did exactly that. Purely, then, as a very personal solo record from a singer-songwriter who had co-led a group, could *Danger in the Past* instead be considered Robert's *Plastic Ono Band*?

> **RF:** I know what you mean. The band I'd started with Grant had broken up. These were turbulent times. I was going through changes as turbulent as the break-up, including being freshly in love, and I felt a terrific sense of freedom and excitement. Liberation even. I was going to tell a whole story over an album. Sides One and Two were going to be mine. All the songs were going to count to something greater than their sum. And without me almost knowing it, a story was embedded in the album, and the sequencing of the album outlined it. Does that make it *Plastic Ono Band*? Maybe.

For what it's worth, here is the track listing of the unmastered Circus *Freakchild* CD: *Broadway Brides / I Love You Still / The House of Snakes / I've Been Looking for Somebody / I Know What It's Like Without You / Easy Come Easy Go / Nowhere by Any Other Name / It Had to Be Me / Running the Risk of Losing You / Is This What You Call Change / I Have Dropped* (extra track).[5] To me, it doesn't really satisfy as a collection, and should you be so inclined, there are many options to choose from in making your own. Have at it – but all these decades later, there seems no point in chasing down the lost *Freakchild*, except out of historical curiosity. The true seventh Go-Betweens album appeared in the year 2000, when the intermission ended.

10 Mythologies

The future is not what it used to be. Nor, in terms of Western pop culture, is the past. The present moment is one of continually redefined nostalgia, when legacy catalogue items may be reissued in many expensive configurations, and vinyl records are prized by some consumers as much for their hipster value as for the music in their grooves.

That's the old fogey argument, however, and none of it matters. Whether you find the music on a playlist or a platter, discovery is always the point. Passionate fandom remains an essential part of the pop music ecosystem today, as much as when Grant McLennan would walk around the campus at the University of Queensland with a prized Monkees LP under his arm. In those days, the love of a band, displayed in this fashion, could make and cement connections between people. Robert Vickers recalls that when he arrived in London in 1983 to join the Go-Betweens, Grant asked him if he still liked the Monkees. They both still did; it was a kind of secret handshake.[1]

Grant's own fandom – for all kinds of art, in all kinds of media – was a huge part of his identity. After Robert Forster's show at the Royal Festival Hall in London on 8 September 2008, the merchandise stand carried a red T-shirt emblazoned with the name 'McLennan' set in off-white, in the style of the famous Monkees 'guitar' logo. Reader, I bought one.

In our age of streaming, releasing music on physical formats remains both worthwhile and meaningful, and many independent artists take an artisanal approach to their own reissues, crafting them with genuine care. The three *'G' Stands for Go-Betweens* boxed sets emerged out of a desire to present the band's music as well as possible. It feels personal, this curation, a duty and a pleasure for all involved.

The same is true of the Robert Forster solo reissues on Needle Mythology. They come from a place of love, inspired by the longstanding fandom of one individual, and neither nostalgia nor commerce is entirely the point. Forster himself is on hand to ensure that these releases, for which he appears truly grateful, are of a suitably high standard.

Pete Paphides, the fan in question, is an accomplished journalist, memoirist and curator. He co-founded the Needle Mythology record label when he realized that many of the albums he wanted in his collection had never been released on vinyl. Named after a single by Stephen Duffy – presiding genius of indie-folk outfit The Lilac Time and founding vocalist of Duran Duran – Needle Mythology has released all four of Robert Forster's 1990s solo records with the utmost respect for the artist and his work. The packaging is superb, each LP including new sleeve notes by Robert, and a 7" single containing extra tracks. The remastering has been done sensitively in a process of restoration rather than reimagining. If you're looking to buy a copy of *Danger in the Past* today, the Needle Mythology release is the one to go for. When I asked Robert about how the reissue came about, he was enthusiastic to discuss it.

RF: I started to do interviews with Pete Paphides. And we got on very well. Then Pete suggested it. We'd been talking. I don't know when I first met Pete. Well, I do. He'd met us as a sixteen-year-old boy on the *16 Lovers Lane* tour. He was interviewing Lindy, and I walked in. In Birmingham. So, I had met him when he was a teenager. And then we started to talk, I think it was in mid-2016, something like that. I started to do radio stations. That's right. He was on Radio Soho. And we just hit it off amazing. He was someone I could talk to and someone I find fascinating. He's always got a very unique way of looking at things, Pete. And then he set up this label and he asked me, and they were really going to do it well. I was thrilled that the album was gonna get a second life. I was very happy it got reissued, very happy. And *Calling from a Country Phone* and *Beautiful Hearts* and *Warm Nights*. Very, very happy. They jump out of the '90s and suddenly here we are in 2024, and they're there again in beautiful packaging. The remastering was done at Abbey Road. It's all quality all the way, and I'm very, very happy about it.

PC: The reissue of *Danger in the Past* contains two bonus tracks, the first version of 'Falling Star' – previously released on the *Intermission* set – and 'The Land that Time Forgot'. Was there much more material recorded during the sessions?

RF: There were no other songs. 'Justice' I probably wrote last, and perhaps 'Falling Star' was very fresh. We ran out of time on that in Hansa, and it could have been good, a great version. But I am kind of glad we didn't finish it. The album was done. And in a way, 'Falling Star' was the start of the next chapter. 'The Land That Time Forgot' is a B-side I like because it's not a 'big' song, but right in its own shape and very much captures the world I was in, writing the album's songs.

PC: The completed 'Falling Star' appears on *Calling from a Country Phone*, and the earlier, sparer version was set aside. Could that song be considered a bridge between the two records?

RF: Yeah. It is. We tried that. To me, 'Falling Star' – which addresses more the break-up of the Go-Betweens – I didn't think it fit. I think the nine songs on the album have a mystery and a oneness that I was happy to stay with.

* * *

For Pete Paphides, there was no question of these reissues being anything other than a labour of love. As a teenage fanzine editor in 1986, he had interviewed Lindy Morrison after his older brother Aki had met her at a gig and told her about Pete's interest in the band. Lindy had said that Pete could just turn up backstage the next night at the show in Birmingham, and she'd talk to him if he wanted an interview for his 'zine. He went out and bought *Liberty Belle and the Black Diamond Express*, released that week, to familiarize himself with the new songs.

PC: What happened when you arrived backstage to meet Lindy?

PP: I turned up, nervous as hell. I couldn't get the questions out of my mouth, and in the end, Lindy pretty much interviewed herself to save me the embarrassment. So, I sat there and occasionally made noises while she just answered all the questions that she thought I'd come to ask. Then, halfway through, Robert walked into the dressing room in a very classically loose Robert manner. I don't recall him even saying anything. He walked into the changing room where the interview was happening – a little bit like when you go to see the giraffes at London Zoo and they just casually walk out of their enclosure and sit down; he sat down cross-legged and just joined in. And so that was the first time I met him, a couple of months shy of my seventeenth birthday.

PC: An interview with Lindy was a good start to your relationship with the Go-Betweens.

PP: After that, I became more and more of a fan and bought all those records. By the time they'd broken up, I had everything. I had the compilation, *1978–1990*. *16 Lovers Lane* came out around the time I was madly falling in love for the first time, and that album was kind of the soundtrack to that. Then I just carried on.

PC: What did you make of Robert's first album at the time?

PP: *Danger in the Past* I thought was just such a stylish and profound record to go solo with. I loved everything about it. The photograph on the front, Mick Harvey's production, I just thought was so fabulous for what Robert's songs sounded like. He created this wonderful ornamentation for these songs, which I still love to this day. I mean, I think Mick Harvey is such a brilliant producer and arranger, and he really suited those songs – the feeling of taking stock, the feeling of saying goodbye to one part of his life and saying hello to another. Often, in certain songs, it almost sounded like it's happening all at once. It was deep – the record was deeper than I was at that point. I would have been about twenty-one. I had to stretch out emotionally to inhabit the place where this record was. And so, I've always loved it.

PC: Over the years, did your relationship with Robert's music develop and deepen?

PP: Robert's one of those artists who I just sort of trust him totally. I just want to know what he's up to. And like all of our favourite artists, we enter into a kind of correspondence with them. Once that trust is there, once they're really part of our lives, a new album from them is just like getting a letter in the post from one of your best friends who's moved far away. And some letters are better than others, but you don't sit there and grade them. You're just really happy that they wrote you a letter. That's how I feel about Robert's music. Years later, when I'd been a music journalist for decades and I was still as much of a fan as I ever was, I thought, let's try and start a label to give some records the releases that they really deserve. And I wasn't thinking about *Danger in the Past* at that point, as that had already come out on vinyl but sadly the ensuing solo albums had not. I thought that needed to be corrected. But then I thought, let's just do them all. Let's do them all as well as possible, put in extra tracks, make them more beautiful than ever, and so we had to do *Danger in the Past*. We couldn't do the others and not do that one. I wanted it to be part of a set that you could collect.

PC: Did you set up the label specifically to put out Robert Forster's records?

PP: Not really, but Robert was on my mind. I thought someone needed to put out *Calling from a Country Phone* and *I Had a New York Girlfriend* and *Warm Nights* on vinyl. Someone *had* to do that. *Warm Nights* had come out on vinyl, but very few copies existed. And I knew Robert wasn't happy with the track listing and a couple of versions of songs he'd put on there. I had a bit of a relationship with Robert at that point because I'd interviewed him subsequently. He'd been on this radio show I do for Soho Radio in London. And sometimes I have guests on. I had Robert on for the whole two hours, just shooting the breeze and playing records. And it went so well that at the end of it he said, 'I'm in town in six months, let's just do it again'. He's since become the most regular guest I've ever had on my show because we just kinda hang out.

PC: How did the reissues come about?

PP: A couple of things happened. Robert was promoting his book *Grant & I*, and he asked if I wanted to host some events with him. We did one at Nottingham Rough Trade, one in Rough Trade East in London, and a ticketed event in the Shaw Theatre in London. We went on a bit of a road trip between the Nottingham event and the London events and had such a fine time. He's such a great prose writer – *The 10 Rules of Rock and Roll* and *Grant & I*. He's just a great stylist. He doesn't even get close to a cliché at any time. He instinctively understands what you need to stay away from as a writer. Which is one of those skills that's borderline unteachable. If you don't feel that in your guts, I think that's a hard thing to teach. And at the time I was writing my own book [*Broken Greek*], a sort of childhood memoir about music and identity, a love letter to pop and what it can do to put you on your path in life. We talked a lot about stuff that ended up being in my book and in his book. And I guess we just kind of became friends, really. I told him that I'd like to start a label and had an idea that I'd like to put out those solo albums. And then when the label got up and running, one of the first records we put out was *I Love My Friends* by Stephen Duffy. On that record, which also had never come out on vinyl before, we used the opportunity to correct a few things that Stephen hadn't been happy with.

PC: All sorts of pressures – release dates, label interference, second-guessing – can lead to an album being released but not entirely finished to the artist's satisfaction. It's rare that they get a chance to revisit and refine the work. What was the situation with Stephen Duffy?

PP: He'd been pressurized into taking a couple of songs off and replacing them with would-be singles that really stuck out because they were produced by a different person. Stephen corrected that so it was the record that he always wanted it to be. And so, Robert knew this was an option. We didn't need to do it with *Danger in the Past* because it's perfect as it is, but we did include a single of B-sides. There's an alternate version of 'Falling Star'. And we thought let's do everything. Let's just make it as beautiful to look at as it is to listen to, and if it costs a bit extra, well, anyone who knows this album is not going to begrudge it because you just want it to exist in its best possible form. We remastered it at Abbey Road. I mean, we did everything. So now when you put it on, it's the best version of the record that it can possibly be. We aimed to make the new version better sonically than the old version. That's what we were going for. The second record, the follow-up, *Calling from a Country Phone*, our version is almost unrecognizable compared to the original. It brought it into another dimension. It's supposed to be a sort of basic rock and roll album, and you wouldn't really hear that in the original version, but when Sean Magee had finished with it . . . Sean Magee, who remastered it, understood exactly what was in the album that needed to be brought out.

PC: Did you have any input into the remastering?

PP: No, I left the mastering with Sean. He's remastered everyone. It would have been nonsense if I'd gone in there like a backseat driver. We did two albums at that one time; we did *Danger* and *Calling from a Country Phone* and Sean was completely upfront. He said when you have a record that's as well produced as this, you really don't need to do anything to it. 'I've done very little to it', he said. 'I've brightened it up a bit but honestly, who am I to correct what Mick Harvey did? Mick has done an absolutely brilliant job.' So, Sean has just optimized it for vinyl release and given it a bit more depth and brightness. *Calling from a Country Phone* is the one where he did all the fancy footwork. It was a very kind of bleached-out sound that it had. There was no depth to it at all. So, Sean rebuilt it as best as he could, and Robert was blown away by the result. With *Danger*, it was very much 'if it ain't broke don't fix it'.

PC: And Robert – was he present at the sessions?

PP: He was, yes, he wouldn't have missed it for the world. He happened to be in the country when it was booked into Abbey Road to be mastered. I think he was working with Matt, the designer, on the third volume of the *'G' Stands for Go-Betweens* box sets. We had a productive few days.

PC: Looking back on the experience, did you achieve what you wanted with the reissues?

PP: Yes, and it's lovely to see Robert gain all this appreciation. Speaking as someone who runs a label, in this climate it's hard to sell 1,500 vinyl albums by an artist who isn't close to being a household name. But you can do it with Robert because there are 1,500 people in the world who will proudly purchase everything that Robert does, and that's because of who he is and what he does and the standards to which he holds himself. That whole thing about never meeting your heroes or never entering into a working arrangement with your heroes, that doesn't apply to Robert. No aspect of working with him has ever been anything less than a delight.

PC: What else did you get up to? I know you developed a muesli around that time.

PP: Do you know about that, the breakfast cereal we worked on [Spring Grain]?[2] On the same trip, Robert and I went to the muesli factory where they presented various prototypes based on the recipe that he'd sent them. And we ate various kinds of muesli recipes – well, they were all his recipe but with different proportions – until we found one that we were happy to go into production with, and that happened on the same weekend that *Danger in the Past* was remastered. Can you imagine, the sixteen-year-old me, who could barely string two words together when he walked into that dressing room, is suddenly in a muesli factory making a Robert-Forster-branded signature muesli. What way do you even begin? Life is just fucking weird sometimes, it's wonderful. I get to put out hopefully the best versions of those records that will exist, and I don't think they can be improved upon, and I'm really proud of that.

11 Needle drops

Pete Paphides and I went from discussing the story of the remaster to some of the individual songs on the album.

PC: What did you make of *Danger in the Past* when you first heard it?

PP: *Danger in the Past*, weirdly, appeared at the right time in my life. I was kind of slightly between one life and not quite ready to start another. I was in university in West Wales and didn't know if I had any kind of a future. I heard 'Baby Stones' before I heard the rest of the album because it came out as a single and it's just, there's a levity to it, a kind of playfulness. It's almost like he can't quite believe he's falling in love, he never thought he'd fall in love again and then: *Oh, here it is, it's happening* – and he's almost amused by it. And when you find the one, you can be a bit flirty, and you can be a bit playful, and it just feels like 'oh this is just comfortable'. It's not actually the most dramatic thing ever, it's just kind of snug and right and that's what that song reminds me of. It's witty too because it's got the elements of 'you don't want to be with him'.

PC: The confidence to write such a song must come from somewhere. Either it was already there in Robert's personality, or he had grown as a writer and was now able to pull it off.

PP: I've said this to Robert's face, and this is not meant to be any kind of an insult, but one of the best things I like about him is that you can tell he was loved as a child. And because he owns his eccentricity so confidently, and he's one of those people who are always going to be kind of OK, even when he's on his uppers. I don't think Robert ever believed that he wasn't charming. He knows he's charming. And weirdly, that doesn't make him less charming. Usually, it does make you less charming if you know it, but Robert has somehow found a way to neutralize that. I don't know how he does it. I think it's just, when you're secure, when you've had that security, but also, you've found your passions and you know you're so lucky to have found your passions – because he could have come out very differently. His self-confidence comes from having been unconditionally loved by at least one or two people at all points in his life. He's just a deeply charming man.

PC: What other songs stood out for you? 'The River People' is about Robert's love for the painting *Tritons*. It feels like a folk song and has been likened to The Band. 'Heart Out to Tender' is more nakedly about Robert's personal life at the time. It has a less straightforward arrangement – more playful.

PP: I was listening to 'Heart Out to Tender' and thinking what a strangely, quintessentially Robert-ish way of singing that melody that is. That arrangement, I don't know if it was Mick's arrangement or if Mick was working to Robert's instruction. I was thinking about the actual melody, what the melody and chords do, and in my head it metamorphosed into a completely different version somewhere between John Lennon doing '#9 Dream' and 'Sun King' by The Beatles. It had that kind of floaty, beatific kind of thing, because that's what the melody and the lyric do. It has this kind of brushes-on-snares, this brilliant sort of slightly eccentric arrangement. To me, it's probably the most eccentric song on the album, but actually there's a very beautiful, sweet, dreamy song hidden in this slightly almost jazzy arrangement. There's a looseness to it. I was thinking about 'Leave Here Satisfied'. What do you think that song is about?

PC: It's a song about Grant, in which Robert visits him after the break-up of the band and finds him in a pretty bad way. But it's also one of those lyrics where he never quite worked out what else it may be about.

PP: Of course, that happens. I love the feeling it has of going back to a place that was once familiar and where you once felt at home. And actually, anything about that place that used to make you feel that way – that warmth – is either not there, or it's changed, or maybe a little bit frightening as a result of that. I guess it's about the passage of time.

PC: You can't go home again. That feeling comes across especially strongly in 'Danger in the Past', too.

PP: Yes. That really spoke to me, particularly in the title track. Obviously, it has that double meaning that the danger that could have once undermined me is now in the past, and it's a relief to be safe. But also, the past can threaten you; the past can come back and swallow you up, the demons of your past life. I just love that song. It's such a profound song, and it's sung by someone who is relatively young. At the time, Robert seemed like a much older person to me. I mean, he was, what, thirty-three or something? That's astonishing to me. Happiness at that age, contentment – it's fragile at any age. He wasn't a father yet, he'd been ill, his future was not a done deal. I imagine he didn't understand how traumatic the break-up of the Go-Betweens was. Because often you don't, straight away. You think you can just walk away from things. You never can, really. In Kriv

Stenders' documentary *Right Here*, you can see that Lindy's been through a whole process regarding the Go-Betweens, and it's seemingly taken her decades to resolve. I love all those things about that record, and because of that, when you hear a happy song on *Danger in the Past*, it doesn't feel trite; it doesn't feel thrown away.

PC: It doesn't feel out of place at all, that happiness, because the journey to get to it works as a narrative progression. It's a complete story arc.

PP: It feels earned. I interviewed Kristin Hersh for *Melody Maker* when I was twenty-four, and she said she never understood it when people think there's anything throwaway about happy songs, or there's anything lighter, that a happy song is more lightweight than a song that isn't happy. When humans feel happiness, it's intense because humans have consciousness and they know it's only here for a little while; it's all in perpetual jeopardy. So, I definitely hear that in, say, 'I've Been Looking for Somebody' or 'Justice'.

PC: There have been times in my life when *Danger in the Past* has offered comfort or a sense of companionship. Did these songs resonate with you personally at all?

PP: I had this amazing experience when my wife and I were much younger. We decided to spontaneously drive out of London to West Wales. It was off-season so we didn't even know where we were going to stay. We ended up in Aberystwyth. We went through this awful storm. It felt like every kind of weather you could imagine. It was practically a blizzard through this really intimidating West Wales scenery, and we were listening to *This is the Sea* by the Waterboys. It culminates in that incredible title track. My windscreen wipers were on full, and I still couldn't see properly, and then about a minute before we get there the weather just completely stops and we see the twinkling harbour lights of Aberystwyth and Mike Scott goes, 'Behold, the sea'. And that's how I think of 'I've Been Looking for Somebody', to just have the person that you love next to you – it could be in a remote shack in the middle of nowhere. Or a farmhouse in Germany. That relief, that sense of 'Oh my God, please don't let this change. I don't need anything else. I don't need my books. I don't need my records. This is just fine'. That's what I get from that song.

12 Portraits of the artist

The cover of *Danger in the Past* replicates a famous photograph of James Joyce playing a guitar, with Robert Forster in place of the author. This is in keeping with the visually literate sensibility he has displayed from the beginning. At various times he has sported the so-called Blake Carrington hairstyle, the American-career-scuppering dress and the canary yellow suit in which he performed on tour in the 1990s. He's claimed Samuel Beckett as an influence on his sartorial style (and namechecked him in a song, 'I Want to be Quiet' on *Calling from a Country Phone*). And he has published at least two amusing articles on hair care.[1] Image has often been an essential part of his act.

As for this portrait of the artist, what does the cover of *Danger in the Past* tell us about the importance of literature to his songwriting? Nothing at all is one answer. It could be just a picture that appealed to him. Or it might be a recognition of his kinship with Joyce, who was also a musician, more usually seen at a piano than with the guitar in the original shot.[2] A musical wordsmith if ever there was one, Joyce once shared a stage with Count John McCormack. Perhaps with this cover, Robert is genuflecting to his creative forebears.

Literature has at times informed his music, Irish literature at that, and not only when poet Marian Stout wrote the words for 'When People are Dead'. Or when another Go-Betweens song,

'The House That Jack Kerouac Built', refers to her: 'reading me poetry that's Irish and so black'.

In 2015, Robert played at the National Concert Hall in Dublin for an event marking W. B. Yeats' 150th birthday, *Blood and the Moon: A Provocation on Yeats*.[3] Also appearing was his good friend Cathal Coughlan, the singer with Microdisney and Fatima Mansions. Anna Calvi, Paul Muldoon and several others were there too, to perform works inspired by the poet. 'Crazy Jane on the Day of Judgement', Robert's adaptation of Yeats' poem of almost the same name, later appeared on *Inferno*.

Of course, Robert had begun his creative life inspired by books. During their time at the University of Queensland, he and Grant studied Irish authors: Joyce, Synge, O'Casey and others. He spoke about this to Ed Power of the *Irish Times* in 2023,[4] the day before his show at the Button Factory, Dublin, in support of *The Candle and the Flame*:

> When I went to university it was like every other writer was Irish. Obviously Dublin is not as isolated as Brisbane. But the fact you could build an artistic vision out of the city you lived in was absolutely fascinating.

Ed Power took up the theme:

> Forster and McLennan had been struck by the confidence with which James Joyce and others wrote about Dublin. They had made it the centre of their world. If they could do that with a rainy city on the edge of Europe, what was to stop the Go-Betweens from similarly embracing obscure, provincial Brisbane as their muse? All the inspiration they needed was, they realised, right there on their doorstep.

Figure 12.1 James Joyce Plays the Guitar, *Trieste, 1915. Photographed by Ottocaro Weiss (1896–1971).*

James Joyce Plays the Guitar (1915), the inspiration for Robert's album cover, was taken in Trieste by Joyce's friend Ottocaro Weiss. The small guitar in the photograph (Figure 12.1) has been kept at the Joyce Tower Museum in Dublin since 1966 and was restored by lutenist Gary Southwell for a series of lunchtime recitals during Bloomsday Week in Dublin in 2012.[5] It's one of those otherwise unremarkable objects made notable by the fact of who owned it. Speculation aside, the real story of that cover is simple enough. Robert told *Uncut*,

> I came across a photo of James Joyce in a library in Ravensburg University, where my wife was studying. Joyce looks a bit like my grandfather, so I decided to replicate the photo for the cover and make no mention of it; just send it out in the world and see what people made of it.[6]

When Ned Raggett reviewed the album for *AllMusic*, he seemed unaware of the cover's link to the author of *Ulysses*:

> certainly the cover photo, black and white with him dressed in a neat suit, looks like it could have been taken somewhere in rural America circa 1920.[7]

Raggett was on to something nevertheless; the photo might easily be mistaken for an image of some Dustbowl bluesman, and Joyce would likely have approved of such a misapprehension.

Robert had a portrait of his own made in 2019 – now the cover of his ninth album *Strawberries* – painted by an artist who uses the name 'what'. The artist won the Doug Moran Prize for this work that, according to the judges, embodies 'the endless possibilities of portraiture and painting'.[8] It was the third time 'what' had painted Robert, whom he described as:

> so important to me as a baby artist in Australia. Great music. Wearing lipstick, wearing dresses.[9]

Preferring to remain elusive, the artist declines to reveal his birth name. This carries into his art, as the painting is, according to the prize judges,

> intriguing for its lack of solid form, and for the way in which the subject hovers on the canvas like a vibrating aura. He is like a Technicolor apparition; neither concrete shape nor exact likeness.[10]

Also a classical guitarist, 'what' perhaps identifies with the soul of his musician subject. He was a finalist in the 2017 Archibald Prize for an earlier portrait of Robert, in which the singer stands in a shirt and blue trousers against a red-brick wall, one hand in his pocket.[11] The less clearly delineated 2019 picture seems a pretty good indication of the kind of portrait 'what' might have made of James Joyce could time travel ever be possible outside of art itself.

The artist known as 'what' is not the first to represent Robert. Melbourne artist Jenny Watson's triptych in oils, *Robert, Lindy, Grant* (1981), graces the sleeve of *Send Me a Lullaby* and was acquired by the National Portrait Gallery of Australia in Canberra.[12] Anne Wallace, a Brisbane artist, depicted him in her painting, *The Go-Betweens* (2001), which the Queensland University of Technology Art Museum bought in 2009.[13]

Maybe the clearest portraits we have of Robert Forster come not in visual art but in the music that he makes. Every song on *Danger in the Past* bears this out. His 2023 record *The Candle and the Flame* completes a journey towards unadorned lyrical truth that began as far back as 'Lee Remick'. The lyrics on that album are inadvertently prescient. The intimacy of its recording while Karin underwent chemotherapy infuses the album with a vibrant power. This is expressed beautifully in the video for 'She's a Fighter', in which Robert, Karin and their children Louis and Loretta sit and play music together as a family.

13 A classic?

The year 1990 was a vintage one for my record collecting disorder. Pixies released *Bossanova*, which felt like that 'difficult second album', although it was their third or fourth, depending on how you count 1987's mini-LP *Come on Pilgrim*. Their label, 4AD, continued its astonishing run of quality, releasing Ultra Vivid Scene's *Joy 1967–1990*, the Breeders' *Pod*, Lush's *Gala*, His Name Is Alive's *Livonia*, Dead Can Dance's *Aion* and Cocteau Twins' *Heaven or Las Vegas*, all of which I bought and loved. They Might Be Giants' *Flood*, Mazzy Star's *She Hangs Brightly* and Pet Shop Boys' *Behaviour* also joined my shelves that year. Lloyd Cole's eponymous album, too. Going out on his own after the Commotions, Cole followed a similar trajectory to Robert's – though it is to be hoped a less traumatic one – ending the band he'd co-founded, moving to another country and recording his solo debut with a crack team of sympathetic musicians whose work he admired.

It was also the year of Nick Cave and the Bad Seeds' *The Good Son*, on which Robert's backing musicians, producer and studio engineer had all worked not long before. *The Good Son* expanded Cave's musical palette into lighter, lusher territory, an approach that would reach its apotheosis on the Bad Seeds' best album, *The Boatman's Call*, seven years later. New Zealand band the Chills' *Submarine Bells* bore a great title – referring to jellyfish, as depicted on the cover – and a No. 1 song,

'Heavenly Pop Hit', which appealed successfully to the gods of nominative determinism. One of the biggest 1990 albums for listeners of a certain vintage was Lou Reed and John Cale's hatchet-burying tribute to the late Andy Warhol, *Songs for Drella*. Cale had a good year, musically at least, as he also released a pop-focused collaboration with Brian Eno, *Wrong Way Up*. Of the albums mentioned above, Lloyd Cole's debut, some of the 4AD records, *Behaviour* and *Songs for Drella* are those that I most often take out for a spin nowadays along with *The Go-Betweens 1978–1990* and *Danger in the Past*.

Why has Robert's album stayed with me? Lloyd Cole, in *Right Here*, says that he'd rather listen to any Go-Betweens record than an entire solo album by either Robert or Grant. I understand the argument: just as Lennon or McCartney worked better in each other's company, so too with Robert and Grant. But for me, in this case at least, it doesn't hold.

Danger in the Past is one of those records that, if the artist were to remain true to himself, couldn't *not* be made. It came out of a crisis familiar to followers of the hero's journey as defined by Joseph Campbell: when alternative futures present themselves, choosing one shuts down the others. In such a moment sacrifices are made, ties are cut, hearts are broken, and a destiny is accepted: blood on the tracks. As a listener to this album, even if you're unaware of the turmoil that led to its creation, you can detect its presence in the songs.

'Every man for the rest of your life will be less than me', the narrator declares in 'Baby Stones', which is the same risk an artist takes in leaving a group to go solo. It's also the downside to producing a masterwork. 'Every album for the rest of your life.' But take the risk you must; you can't do otherwise.

Danger in the Past doesn't appear in Rolling Stone Australia's 2016 list of the 200 Greatest Australian Albums of All Time. Nor is it on ABC/Triple J's 2010 Countdown of the Hottest Australian Albums, as voted on by 175 music industry figures. The Go-Betweens appear on those lists, with 16 Lovers Lane doing best: #15 on the Rolling Stone Australia list; #84 on the ABC list; and #12 in the book, The 100 Best Australian Albums (2012). The Guardian Australia ran a 'Songs of Brisbane' poll in 2018. The Saints showed strongly with four songs, but the two bands most heavily represented were Powderfinger and the Go-Betweens, with five songs each. 'Streets of Your Town' topped the poll.

Today, the band he came from is more famous than ever – the Go-Between Bridge was named by a public vote, after all – and Robert's own stock is always reaching new heights, but Danger in the Past seems to remain a cult classic rather than an unassailable cultural edifice. The Irish Times reviewed the reissue with an ambivalent note:

> it beggars belief that on initial release Danger in the Past drew comparisons with Bob Dylan's Blood on the Tracks. Forster's style here is crackling Americana and certainly Dylanesque in parts, but the songs aren't there yet. His more recent work has settled, certainly, into a classic phase, but 30 years ago it was embryonic. And yet, as you might expect, there are gorgeous tunes here: the compact likes of The River People, I've Been Looking for Somebody, and Justice are folk-pop standouts on a flawed, inconsistent record.[1]

Ned Raggett at AllMusic wrote of the original release:

> The album is a fine first step away from the constraints of the Go-Betweens and proves that Forster is more than able to go his own way.[2]

Aphoristic Album Reviews had this to say:

> *Danger in the Past* is the most loved of Forster's solo albums from the 1990s. With a cache of material left over from the Go-Betweens, Forster already had a strong set of songs. The six strangled minutes of 'Dear Black Dream' are quintessentially Forster, with the memorable line 'Wondering who sings better in the dark / Is it Townes Van Zandt, or is it Guy Clark?' 'Baby Stones' is a fine opener, with the line 'You say, you want to take a lover / Although you're satisfied with me.' Forster's haughty nerviness is one-dimensional without McLennan to balance him, but *Danger in the Past* is still a fine solo debut.[3]

Reviewing *Inferno* in 2019, Andrew Stafford wrote perceptively of Robert's career, placing it in a contemporary context:

> He's also a marathoner, not a sprinter. He's 61 now, with seven solo albums under his belt around the nine he made with the Go-Betweens, and he is one of Australian music's elders. He doesn't sell remotely as many records as Nick Cave, a close peer and friend, or Paul Kelly. On the song Remain, he says, 'I did my good work, knowing it wasn't my time.' The groove of this song is totally relaxed as he speaks of being overlooked and forgotten. Forster doesn't care. Not only is he an optimist, he's supremely self-assured. He knows what he does is good without needing the validation of others . . . While others overtake him, Forster is content to cruise and to observe,

knowing that one day they'll catch up with him – not the other way around.[4]

Stafford is not alone in recognizing Robert's enduring relevance as an artist. In 2023, Lech Blaine wrote in the *Sydney Morning Herald*:

> Being a quiet achiever has some unexpected economic benefits. 'His European tour in 2019 drew bigger crowds than the Go-Betweens ever got,' says Bernard Galbally, Forster's [Australian] manager. 'The audiences listen to his new music. They aren't waiting to hear three hit songs from 40 years ago.'[5]

It seems right that Robert Forster continues to be appreciated by listeners who come for his new songs as well as the classics. Like those Velvet Underground LPs in the Brisbane of his youth, *Danger in the Past* thrives on personal recommendation. I have introduced it to friends who hadn't heard of it and who now hold it in high esteem.

In terms of his contemporaries, *Danger in the Past* is every bit as good as Nick Cave and the Bad Seeds' *The Boatman's Call*. It's up there with David McComb's *Love of Will*, a solo album designed as such, not intended to be played by his band the Triffids, whose circumstances in Perth shared a lot of similarities with those of the Go-Betweens in Brisbane.[6] Robert has spoken about the kinship he and Grant felt with the Triffids.

> We read . . . about this band over in Perth who were into the Velvet Underground and Dylan, and also Talking Heads and Television, and Grant and I went 'okay!' This is years before we met them. We had a feeling about the band before we started

playing shows with them. We played a lot of shows in Australia with the Triffids when they lived in Sydney in the early '80s.[7]

The Triffids' *Born Sandy Devotional* is a cult classic on a par with *Liberty Belle and the Black Diamond Express*, both picked by 'Australia's greatest songwriter'[8] Paul Kelly as his favourite albums. He told the *Sydney Morning Herald* in 2021:

> They had this big impact on me as a songwriter who was only just finding my own way to write songs. I'd been aware of both bands before then, but these were fully realised records from bands at their peak. Every song was its own world, the songwriting was strong on every track, and the production was open. A lot of '80s recordings were often bombastic, but they got it right. Songs full of grandeur and yearning.[9]

Is *Danger in the Past* Robert's greatest album? It may well be. No artist stands still, however, and he has made many excellent records since. *The Evangelist* (2008) shines with emotional resonance: 'Demon Days', one of three co-written with Grant; the elegiac 'From Ghost Town'; and the title track, which is about Karin. *The Candle and the Flame* (2023) could reasonably claim top position if one is counting, and I'm not: there are likely three or four 'best' Robert Forster solo albums, depending on who you ask. That said, because it has been such a friend over the years, the one I return to time and again is *Danger in the Past*. It's a classic.

Discography

Robert Forster's solo albums of the 1990s have been reissued by Needle Mythology in limited editions on vinyl, each accompanied by a 7" single containing extra tracks; the CDs place the bonus tracks after the main album. The five albums that Robert released after the second ending of the Go-Betweens are readily available, and all are recommended.

The Go-Betweens' first six albums have been re-released quite a few times over the years, notably by Beggars Banquet in 1996, in a uniform edition of remastered CDs. The 2-CD releases from 2002 and 2004 are the ones to go for if extra tracks are your bag. The second-phase Go-Betweens released single-disc editions of their albums on CD with the exception of *Oceans Apart*, which in one configuration came with a bonus disc of live tracks taken from *Live in London*. That record of their performance at the Barbican in 2004 reveals Robert and Grant in full flight and is an essential part of their discography. It was released on CD in 2005 and later as a download included with the third *'G' Stands for Go-Betweens* box set. If you have the means, and can find them, those Domino sets are recommended. They're likely to remain the best presentation of the Go-Betweens' catalogue in physical form. A note on *Oceans Apart*: early pressings suffered from distortion due to heavy compression applied in the mastering, the dreaded so-called brickwalling. The album remained blighted until its reissue in 2024 in the third 'G' Stands for Go-Betweens set, for which it was remixed successfully by its producer Mark Wallis. *Oceans Apart*, the final Go-Betweens studio album, can finally be heard in all its pristine glory.

Grant McLennan's solo albums are worth hearing not simply because they are very good. For our interest, they contain tracks that would have otherwise appeared on the intended folk duo with Robert and because they illustrate just how different these songwriters were when working away from each other. Jack Frost, Grant's duo with Steve Kilbey, shows us how he collaborated with someone who wasn't Robert. Far Out Corporation is Grant's other band project, a supergroup featuring future Go-Between Adele Pickvance, Ross McLennan (no relation) and Ian Haug of Powderfinger.

Cleopatra Wong is Lindy Morrison and Amanda Brown's band, formed after the Go-Betweens; it heads in the direction of electropop. Amanda Brown's *Eight Guitars* is her first non-soundtrack solo record and is heartily recommended.

Robert Forster

Danger in the Past (Beggars Banquet, 1990 / Needle Mythology, 2020).

Calling from a Country Phone (Beggars Banquet, 1993 / Needle Mythology, 2020).

I Had a New York Girlfriend / Beautiful Hearts (Beggars Banquet, 1994 / Needle Mythology, 2024).

Warm Nights (Beggars Banquet, 1993 / Needle Mythology, 2024).

The Evangelist (Yep-Roc / Tuition, 2008).

Songs to Play (Universal Music Australia / Tapete Records, 2015).

Inferno (Tapete Records, 2019).
The Candle and the Flame (Tapete Records, 2023).
Strawberries (Tapete Records, 2025).

The Go-Betweens

Send Me A Lullaby (Missing Link, 1981 / Rough Trade, 1982 / 2-CD, Circus, 2002).
Before Hollywood (Rough Trade, 1983 / 2-CD, Circus, 2002).
Spring Hill Fair (Sire, 1984 / 2-CD, Circus, 2002).
Liberty Belle and the Black Diamond Express (Beggars Banquet, 1986 / 2-CD, Lo-Max, 2004).
Tallulah (Beggars Banquet, 1987 / 2-CD, Lo-Max, 2004).
16 Lovers Lane (Beggars Banquet, 1988 / 2-CD, Lo-Max, 2004).
The Friends of Rachel Worth (Circus / Jetset, 2000).
Bright Yellow Bright Orange (Circus / Jetset, 2003).
Oceans Apart (Lo-Max / EMI, 2005).

G. W. / Grant McLennan

Watershed (Beggars Banquet, 1991).
Fireboy (Beggars Banquet, 1992).
Horsebreaker Star (Beggars Banquet, 1994).
In Your Bright Ray (Beggars Banquet, 1997).

Jack Frost

Jack Frost (RedEye Records / Polydor, 1990 / Arista, 1991).
Snow Job (Beggars Banquet / Karmic Hit, 1996).

Far Out Corporation

FOC (Polydor, 1998).

Cleopatra Wong

Egg (rooArt / Warner, 1992).
Cleopatra's Lament (rooArt / Warner, 1993).

Amanda Brown

Eight Guitars (self-released via Bandcamp, 2023).

Compilations

The Go-Betweens 1978–1990 (Beggars Banquet, 1990).
16 Lovers Lane Acoustic Démos (Les Inrockuptibles, 1996).
Bellavista Terrace: Best of the Go-Betweens (Beggars Banquet, 1999).
78 'til 79 – The Lost Album (Jetset, 1999).
Intermission: The Best of the Solo Recordings 1990–1997 (Beggars Banquet, 2007).
Quiet Heart: The Best of the Go-Betweens (EMI, 2012).

Boxed sets

'G' Stands for Go-Betweens: The Go-Betweens Anthology.
Volume 1 (Domino, 2014).
Volume 2 (Domino, 2019).

Volume 3 (Domino, 2024).

Live albums

Live on Snap (included with the special edition of *Bellavista Terrace*, 1999).

Live in London (Tag 5 Records, 2005).

Live at the Tivoli (included with *That Striped Sunlight Sound* DVD, 2006).

Vienna Burns (included with *Quiet Heart: The Best of the Go-Betweens*, 2012).

Fountains of Youth (part of *'G' Stands for Go-Betweens* Volume 2, 2019).

Nachtmix Live (part of *'G' Stands for Go-Betweens* Volume 3, 2024).

DVDs

Tutty, J., dir. (2005) *That Striped Sunlight Sound*. Germany: Tuition.

Stenders, K., dir. (2017) *The Go-Betweens: Right Here*. Australia: Essential Media.

Notes

Preface

1. Robert Forster's Go-Betweens song 'Here Comes a City' (2005) asks: Why do people who read Dostoevsky / Look like...Dostoevsky?
2. On winning the W.H. Smith Award in 1966.
3. From *Lady Windermere's Fan* (1892).

Chapter 1

1. Edwyn Collins was an early champion of the Go-Betweens. His label Postcard Records released their single 'I Need Two Heads' in 1980.
2. Microdisney's principals went on to take different musical paths, Cathal Coughlan in the Fatima Mansions and Telefís; and Sean O'Hagan in the High Llamas.
3. Many of these acts shared members under pseudonyms such as Hollis Golightly and Jangly Rheinhardt.
4. See an interview with Seán McDermott at http://www.cloudberryrecords.com/blog/?p=3391.
5. Author interview, 2024.
6. Jay McInerney's novels in the Calloway series are *Brightness Falls*, *The Good Life* and *Bright, Precious Days*.

7 'Baby Stones' on *Danger in the Past* and 'Over Stones for You' on Grant's album, *Watershed*.

8 C. Walker, *Stranded: Australian Independent Music 1977–1992* (Sydney: The Visible Spectrum, 1996, revised and expanded ed. 2021), p. 255.

9 C. Walker, reviewing *The Go-Betweens 1978–1990*, *Rolling Stone Australia*, January 1991.

10 This was thirteen years before Lloyd Cole's 'Impossible Girl' but not before a host of women songwriters. Dolly Parton, Kate Bush and more have produced enough period songs to fill an album in the *Now That's What I Call Music* series.

11 Selected in 2001 by the Australasian Performing Right Association as one of the Top 30 Australian songs of all time.

12 David Byrne made his album – a masterpiece of understatement whose sound was inspired by the Dirty Dozen Brass Band of New Orleans – to provide interlude material, or knee plays, for Robert Wilson's gargantuan, unfinished opera *the CIVIL warS: a tree is best measured when it is down*.

13 The Confessional movement in poetry gets its name from 'Poetry as Confession', an article by M.L. Rosenthal, reviewing Robert Lowell's collection *Life Studies*, in the *Nation*, 19 September 1959.

14 Did Robert and Grant ever consider calling a Go-Betweens LP *Hartley*?

15 L.P. Hartley, *The Go-Between* (London: Hamish Hamilton, 1953).

16 W. Faulkner, *Requiem for a Nun* (New York: Random House, 1951).

Chapter 2

1. Male homosexual acts were legalized in Ireland on 24 June 1993, when, after campaigning by David Norris and others, leftover colonial British-era legislation was repealed. The oft-floated idea that the reason female homosexual acts were never illegal was because Queen Victoria refused to believe in them, is unsupported by the historical record.

2. John McGahern and Edna O'Brien were two of the writers persecuted.

3. See Charles J. Haughey's infamous State of the Nation address on RTÉ Television, 9 January 1980.

4. F. Bongiorno, *The Eighties: The Decade That Transformed Australia* (Melbourne: Black Inc., 2015).

5. See https://oa.anu.edu.au/obituary/bjelkepetersen-sir-johannes-joh-33578.

6. A. Stafford, *Pig City: From the Saints to Savage Garden* (Brisbane: University of Queensland Press, 2004).

7. For more on the Missing Links, see Jon Stratton, 'The Missing Links', in Jon Stratton and Jon Dale with Tony Mitchell (eds), *An Anthology of Australian Albums: Critical Engagements* (London: Bloomsbury, 2020), 9–22.

8. See http://radicaltimes.info/PDF/4ZZZhistory.pdf for a history of 4ZZZ.

9. 'Lindy Morrison, Megan Washington, Regurgitator and More Pick Their Favourite Brisbane Song', *The Guardian*, 4 September 2018.

10. See https://en.wikipedia.org/wiki/Fitzgerald_Inquiry.

11 M. Vavaris and Stephen Green, 'Robert Forster on Brisbane's Punk Scene: It was a New, Fresh, Musical Revolution', *The Music*, 8 April 2024.

12 See https://allpoetry.com/poem/8507389-Advent-by-Patrick-Kavanagh.

13 R. Forster, *Grant & I* (Sydney: Penguin Books Australia, 2016).

14 B. Zuel, https://www.bernardzuel.net/post/2019/05/08/the-dreamer-and-the-strategist-the-last-go-betweens-interview-brings-wind-back-wednesday.

15 http://www.robertforster.net/rfbiography.html.

16 Ibid.

17 T. Thorn, *My Rock'n'Roll Friend* (Edinburgh: Canongate, 2021), p. 29.

18 M. Schafter 'Robert Forster Reflects on 30 Years of Friendship with Go-Betweens Collaborator Grant McLennan', *ABC.net.au*, 24 August 2016.

19 K. Stenders, dir., *The Go-Betweens: Right Here* (Australia: Essential Media, 2017).

20 I. McFarlane, *The Encyclopedia of Australian Rock and Pop* (St. Leonard's: Allen & Unwin, 1999).

21 M. Snow, 'The Gentle Three-Headed Monster', *NME*, 21 August 1982.

22 L. Anderson, 'Smoke Rings', from the album, *Home of the Brave*, Warner Bros., 1986.

23 Interview with Simone Téry, 24 March 1945, in Alfred H. Barr, *Picasso: Fifty Years of his Art* (New York: MoMA, 1946).

24 D. Cohen, 'What's so Controversial About Picasso's Guernica?', *Slate*, 6 February 2003.

25 When the Country (later National) Party first won power in 1957 under Bjelke-Petersen's predecessor Frank Nicklin, it inherited a system of malapportionment from the previous Labor Party government. Nicklin reworked that set-up to benefit the Country and Liberal parties instead.

26 Z. Fitzgerald, *Save Me the Waltz* (New York: Charles Scribner's Sons, 1932).

27 *Nouvelle Vague*, the French New Wave in film, influenced Grant and Robert even as New Waves emerged in both Australian cinema and pop music in Britain.

28 On the *10 Rules of Rock and Roll* book tour. See https://andrewmcmillen.com/2009/11/25/a-conversation-between-robert-forster-and-john-willsteed-november-2009/.

29 See https://dylan.utulsa.edu/442-2/.

30 C. Kellet, 'New Brisbane Bridge Named after Rock Band', *Brisbane Times*, 29 September 2009.

Chapter 3

1 *Grant & I*.

2 Ibid.

3 Michael Fish, designer, pioneered what came to be known as the Peacock Revolution.

4 *Right Here*.

5 Ibid.

6 Ibid.

7. *Casablanca* (Curtiz, 1942), Rick, played by Humphrey Bogart, remarks, "…the problems of three little people don't amount to a hill of beans in this crazy world."
8. *Grant & I*.
9. L. Cohen, 'True Love Leaves No Traces', from *Death of a Ladies' Man* (Warner, 1977).
10. *Grant & I*.
11. *Right Here*.
12. John Willsteed, *Dive For Your Memory* at the State Library of Queensland: https://www.slq.qld.gov.au/blog/dive-your-memory.
13. *Grant & I*.
14. Ibid.
15. Ibid.
16. Ibid.
17. Ibid.
18. Ibid.
19. *Right Here*.
20. T. Thorn, *My Rock'n'Roll Friend* (Edinburgh: Canongate, 2021), p. 60.
21. B. Zuel, 'Go-Betweens and Eurogliders – Two Sides of the 1980s Reviewed', *Sydney Morning Herald*, 20 February 2015.
22. See http://www.abc.net.au/triplej/music_specials/s1407504.htm.
23. See https://www.toppermost.co.uk/the-go-betweens/.
24. See https://www.silentradio.co.uk/02/17/interview-q-a-robert-forster-the-go-betweens/.

25 L. Blaine, 'For the Go-Betweens' Robert Forster, the Beat Goes on Despite "The Situation"', *Sydney Morning Herald*, 26 January 2023.

26 *Right Here*.

27 Ibid.

28 C. Gibson, *The Church's Starfish* (New York: Bloomsbury Academic, 2022).

29 S. Kilbey, *Something Quite Peculiar* (Richmond, Victoria: Hardie Grant Books, 2014).

30 *Grant & I*.

31 The Go-Betweens' comeback album in 2000, *The Friends of Rachel Worth*, features members of Sleater Kinney and Quasi, as well as Adele Pickvance. She and Glenn Thompson of Custard joined a new, permanent line-up for subsequent albums, making a quartet of Robert, Grant, Adele and Glenn. All four had played together on tour in the 1990s.

32 Ibid.

33 To mark the occasion, *Les Inrockuptibles* released a covermount CD, *16 Lovers Lane – Acoustic Démos* on 22 May 1996.

Chapter 5

1 R. Fitzpatrick, 'Ireland in 50 Albums, No 12: *Achtung Baby*, by U2', *Irish Examiner*, 12 April 2023.

2 *Grant & I*.

3 Author interview, 2024.

4 *Right Here*.

5 *Grant & I*.

6 J. Mulvey, 'Robert Forster, Album by Album', *Uncut*, 18 January 2016.

7 See https://theconversation.com/the-end-of-history-francis-fukuyamas-controversial-idea-explained-193225.

Chapter 7

1 *Right Here*.

2 ...in a lyric lifted from 'Baby, Let's Play House', John Lennon quotes this Arthur Gunter song covered by Elvis Presley in 1954. See J. Wenner, *Lennon Remembers* (England: Penguin, 1972), 128.

3 *Grant & I*.

4 Peter Weir's 1977 film *The Last Wave* is both political and mythic. See https://www.tabula-rasa.info/AusHorror/LastWave.html.

5 See Robert's lecture here: https://www.artgallery.nsw.gov.au/art/watch-listen-read/watch/243/.

6 See link in note #94.

7 Dire Straits used part of Brett Whiteley's work *Alchemy* for the cover of their first live album, also called *Alchemy*, in 1985.

8 The Walkabouts, *Satisfied Mind*, Sub Pop, 1993.

9 *I'm Your Fan: The Songs of Leonard Cohen* (1991), produced by *Les Inrockuptibles* and released on EastWest in Europe, features two very different versions of 'Tower of Song', one by Robert Forster, the other by Nick Cave and the Bad

Seeds. See R. Padgett, *I'm Your Fan* (New York: Bloomsbury Academic, 2020).

10 B. Robinson, *Withnail & I – the Original Screenplay* (New York: Bloomsbury, new edition, 1998).

11 *Grant & I*.

12 L. Blaine, *Sydney Morning Herald*, 26 January 2023.

13 Bob Dylan's 1965 single apparently ridicules those who criticised his going electric.

14 This vituperative song on John Lennon's 1971 album, *Imagine*, makes a strange bedfellow with the title track.

15 *Grant & I*.

16 Ibid.

17 Robert Lowell's *Life Studies* (London: Faber, 1959), is one of the most influential poetry collections of the twentieth century.

18 A. Sexton, *Complete Poems* (New York: Ecco, 1999).

19 *American Heritage Dictionary*.

20 J. Mulvey, 'Robert Forster, Album by Album', *Uncut*, 18 January 2016.

21 See https://www.bernardzuel.net/post/years-both-tender-and-brutal-the-robert-forster-interview-part-1.

Chapter 8

1 C. Connolly, *Enemies of Promise* (London: Andre Deutsch, 1938).

2 S. Garret, https://thecreativelife.net/scenius/.

3 J. G. Ballard, *Miracles of Life* (London: Fourth Estate, 2008).

4 V. Woolf, *A Room of One's Own* (London: Hogarth Press, 1929).

5 D. Lynch, *Catching the Big Fish: Meditation, Consciousness, and Creativity* (U.S.: Tarcher, 2006).

6 As recounted by J.G. Ballard – fiction editor of *Ambit* – in the *Paris Review*, issue 94, Winter 1984. Ann Quin's work is highly recommended.

Chapter 9

1 *My Beatles Black Album* (Sky Arts, 2017). See charleshazlewood.com.

2 On the CD *Loving Shocks – Rarities volume 8: 1989*, included in *'G' Stands for Go-Betweens, Volume 3* (2019).

3 didnotchart.blogspot.com, 30 April 2012.

4 Y. Berra, *The Yogi Book* (New York: Workman Publishing, 1988).

5 didnotchart.blogspot.com, 30 April 2012.

Chapter 10

1 *Magnet Magazine*, 8 February 2007 https://magnetmagazine.com/2007/02/08/grant-mclennan-1958-2006/.

2 Spring Grain, a muesli named after the Go-Betweens song 'Spring Rain'.

Chapter 12

1. R. Forster, 'Hair Care with Robert Forster', *Debris* issue 16, Manchester, England, 1987; and 'Hair Care in the Modern Age', *Time Out*, London, 11–18 July, 2001.

2. See *The World of James Joyce: His Life & Work*, produced for RTÉ Television in 1986.

3. Read the titular poem, here: https://www.poetry.com/poem/39297/blood-and-the-moon.

4. E. Power, 'Cathal Coughlan was an Inspiration: Robert Forster on the Go-Betweens' Irish Spirit', *The Irish Times*, 23 March 2023.

5. See https://southwellguitars.co.uk/.

6. J. Mulvey, *Uncut*.

7. See https://www.allmusic.com/album/danger-in-the-past-mw0000317257.

8. S. Convery, 'Doug Moran Prize 2019: Mysterious Artist 'What' Wins $150,000 for Robert Forster Portrait', *The Guardian*, 30 October 2019.

9. Ibid.

10. Ibid.

11. Ibid.

12. Jenny Watson, *Robert, Lindy, Grant*, 1981 (National Portrait Gallery, NSW, 1951–).

13. See https://artguide.com.au/anne-wallace-on-realism-motherhood-and-creating-tension/.

Chapter 13

1. T. Clayton-Lea, *The Irish Times*, 27 March 2020.
2. See https://www.allmusic.com/album/danger-in-the-past-mw0000317257.
3. https://albumreviews.blog/reviews/punk-and-new-wave-reviews/the-go-betweens/.
4. https://www.theguardian.com/music/2019/mar/01/robert-forster-inferno-review-loads-of-atmosphere-and-dry-brisbane-wit.
5. L. Blaine, *Sydney Morning Herald*, 26 January 2023.
6. G. D'Cruz, *Truckload of Sky: The Lost Songs of David McComb* (New York: Bloomsbury Academic, 2025).
7. See https://andrewmcmillen.com/2009/11/25/a-conversation-between-robert-forster-and-john-willsteed-november-2009/.
8. C. Mathieson, 'No One Would Ever Pick This': Australian Musicians Reveal Their Favourite Albums', *Sydney Morning Herald*, 20 November 2021.
9. Ibid.

Bibliography

Bongiorno, F. (2015) *The Eighties: The Decade That Transformed Australia*. Melbourne: Black Inc.

Buskies, G., J. Engelmann, et al. (2023) *Thank You For A Lovely Day: The Go-Betweens Songcomics*. Mainz: Ventil Verlag UG.

Cohen, T. (2023) *Half Deaf, Completely Mad*. Melbourne: Black Inc.

Forster, R. (2009) *The 10 Rules of Rock and Roll: Collected Music Writings 2005-09*. Melbourne: Black Inc.

Forster, R. (2016) *Grant & I*. Sydney: Penguin Books Australia.

Kilbey, S. (2014) *Something Quite Peculiar*. Richmond, Victoria: Hardie Grant Books.

McFarlane, I. (1999) *The Encyclopedia of Australian Rock and Pop*. St. Leonard's: Allen & Unwin.

Nichols, D. (1997, revised and expanded ed. 2011) *The Go-Betweens*. Portland: Verse Chorus Press.

O'Brien, P. (2024) *Nowhere Fast: Brisbane's Punk and Post-punk Scene 1978-1982*. Brisbane: And Also Books.

Paphides, P. (2024) *Broken Greek*. London: Quercus.

Stafford, A. (2004) *Pig City: From the Saints to Savage Garden*. Brisbane: University of Queensland Press.

Thorn, T. (2021) *My Rock'n'Roll Friend*. Edinburgh: Canongate.

Walker, C. (1996, revised and expanded ed. 2021) *Stranded: Australian Independent Music 1977–1992*. Sydney: The Visible Spectrum.

Index

Abbey Road (studios) 56, 102–3
Able Label 18
Acevedo, Amanda 51
Alteglofsheim 27, 29, 30, 65, 68
Anderson, Laurie 19
Armiger, Michael 33

Baby You Know 30, 75
Bad Seeds (Nick Cave)
    Boatman's Call, The 117, 121
    Cohen, Tony produces 31
    Good Son, The 74, 117
    at Hansa 45
    members play on Danger in the Past 46–7
Ballard, J. G. 86
Bäumler, Karin, *see also* Tritons
    Baby You Know, member of 30
    begins relationship with RF 27–30
    Candle and the Flame, The 122
    country music 75
    'Danger in the Past' 53
    'The Evangelist' 80
    'Heart Out to Tender' 71
    marriage to RF 38
    puts on RF's dress 28
    Ravensburg University, studies at 113
Beatles, The 56, 64, 91, 106
Beckett, Samuel 16, 111
Beggars Banquet 9, 31, 55
Berra, Yogi 93
Berry, Bill 27, 61
Birthday Party, the 4, 24, 31, 46, 54
Bjelke-Petersen, Joh 11–13, 15, 21–2, 73
Blood and the Moon 112
Botany sessions 31, 93
Bowie, David 28, 33, 45–6, 48, 67
Boys Next Door, the 31
Brown, Amanda 7, 25, 30, 33–7, 124
Browne, Jackson 17

Bunny, Rupert   66, 68
Byrne, David   5, 9

Calvi, Anna   112
Campbell, Joseph   118
Cash, Johnny   75
Catching the Big Fish   86
Cave, Nick   47, 74, 117, 120–1
Church, The (band)   37
Cinema Papers   18
Clark, Guy   60, 75–6, 79, 120
Climbing Frame   34
Cobain, Kurt   28
Cohen, Leonard   29
Cohen, Tony   31–2
Cole, Lloyd   38, 117, 118
Collins, Edwyn   3, 61
Connolly, Cyril   85
Cooder, Ry   17
Coughlan, Cathal   112
Creedence Clearwater Revival   16
Crime and the City Solution   46

Damned, The   14
Dando, Evan   28
'Danger in the Past' (song lyric)   78
Davis, Éamonn   3, 7
Dexys Midnight Runners   19
Die Haut   47

Dinosaur Jr.   60
Drysdale, Russell   68
Duffy, Stephen   96, 101–2
Duran Duran   96
Dylan, Bob
    Blood on the Tracks   69, 119
    critical comparison with RF   119
    influence on RF   7, 56, 79
    Karin and RF, bonding   89
    'thin wild mercury sound'   24
    Triffids' admiration of   121

Ely, Ben   14

Fagot, John   27
Fatima Mansions   112
Fireboy   32
Fish, Michael   28
Fitzgerald, Zelda   24
Flaubert, Gustave   85–6, 88–9
Forster, Robert (other albums)
    Beautiful Hearts, aka I Had a New York Girlfriend   97, 100
    Calling from a Country Phone   93, 97–8, 100, 103, 111
    Candle and the Flame, The   47, 112, 115, 122

Evangelist, The 80, 112
Inferno 47, 112, 120
Intermission (compilation album) 97
Songs to Play 124
Strawberries 114
Warm Nights 74, 97, 100
4ZZZ (radio station) 13–14
Freakchild (proposed album) 42, 91–4

Gabriel, Peter 77
Galbally, Bernard (manager) 121
Genet, Jean 16, 63
Go-Between, The (Hartley novel) 9
Go-Betweens, The (albums)
 Friends of Rachel Worth, The 93
 Go-Betweens 1978–1990help_outlineTS: Please validate this page number, as it seems like out of range, The 3, 7–8, 99, 118
 'G' Stands for Go-Betweens 96, 103, 123–4
 Liberty Belle and the Black Diamond Express 41, 98, 122
 Live in London 123
 Oceans Apart 76, 93, 123–4
 Send Me a Lullaby 24, 115
 16 Lovers Lane 30–1, 42, 60, 67, 74, 92, 119
Go Between Bridge 25, 119
Godard, Jean-Luc 16, 24
Godots, the 18
Grundl, Erhard 30
Guernica 20

Hansa Tonstudios
 Bakelite organ 82
 effect on sound of record 71
 'Falling Star' 97
 Meistersaal 45, 48–9
 MH and RF recall sessions 51–7
 previous visit by RF 49
 recording sessions begin 45
 recordings progress 47
 studio history 48
Happy Mondays 60
Harvey, Mick 46–7, 59, 71, 82, 99, 103
Hazlewood, Charles 91
Hey, Paulette! 3, 5
Hitchcock, Alfred 48

(*I'm*) *Stranded* 14
Intermission, the 38–9, 93–4

Jack Frost (band) 37, 93, 124
Jagger, Mick 28
James, Etta 64
Joel, Billy 64
Johnson, Bob (manager) 37, 55
Joyce, James 16, 63, 111, 113, 115

Kavanagh, Patrick 16
Kelly, Paul 120, 122
Kerr, John 12
Kilbey, Steve 37, 124
Kniepp, Tony 14
Kuepper, Ed 15, 19

Laughing Clowns, the 24
Lennon, John 59, 72, 91, 106, 118
Lilac Time, The 96
Lowell, Robert 77
Lynch, David 86

Magee, Sean 102
Mamas and the Papas, the 16, 59
McCartney, Paul 91, 118
McComb, David 121
McCormack, Count John 111
McDermott, Seán A. 4–5

McFarlane, Ian 18
McLennan, Grant
   art life, the 87–8
   break-up of the
      Go-Betweens 35–7
   first meets RF 17
   forms Go-Betweens with
      RF 21
   'Leave Here Satisfied',
      subject of 107
   Lindy Morrison's
      drumming 34
   Monkees fandom 95
   Steve Kilbey, forms duo
      with 37
Meisel, Peter 48
Meisel, Thomas 48
Mickey Rourke's Fridge 4
Microdisney 4, 112
Monkees, the 16, 95
Morrison, Lindy
   Cleopatra Wong 124
   dissolution of
      Go-Betweens 36–9
   drumming 33–4
   joins Go-Betweens 23–4
   Pete Paphides
      interview 97–9
Muldoon, Paul 112

Needle Mythology 9, 96, 123
Nolan, Sydney 68

O'Brien, Paul   15
O'Casey, Sean   112
Ono, Yoko   72

Paphides, Pete   79, 96–8, 105
Parameters, the   14
Peel, John   3
Phillips, John   59
Phillips, Kathleen   29
Picasso, Pablo   19–20
Pig City (song)   14
Pixies   7, 33, 60, 117
Plastic Ono Band   72, 91, 94
Plath, Sylvia   9, 77, 79
Pogues, the   57
Pop, Iggy   46
Postcard Records   3, 5, 18, 61
Powderfinger   119, 124
Powell, Colin   20
Preston, Richard   41
Preußen Tonstudios   53
Prine, John   59

Queensland, University of   21, 95, 112
Quin, Ann   86

Race, Hugo   46, 48, 53
Razar   14
Regurgitator   14
R.E.M.   27–9
Richman, Jonathan   16

Robinson, Bruce   69
Rocky Mountain Spotted Fever   27
Rough Trade   4, 101

Saints, The   13–14, 119
Schonell (cinema)   18
Sexton, Anne   9, 77, 79
Smith, Patti   9, 16
Southwell, Gary   113
Spring Grain (muesli)   104
Stafford, Andrew   13–15, 120–1
Starfish (The Church album)   37
Stars of Heaven, the   4
Stenders, Kriv   28, 108
Stiff Little Fingers   14
Stipe, Michael   28
Stout, Marion   111
Striped Sunlight Sound, That   5, 24
Sylvian, David   45
Synge, John Millington   112

Talking Heads   121
Tallulah   30, 35, 41–2
Television (band)   121
Tennant, Gertrude   85
Thatcher, Margaret   51, 69
Thorn, Tracey   17, 33
Triffids, The   4, 37, 121–2

Tritons 66–8, 106
Truffaut, François 24
Two Wimps and a Witch 24

U2 5, 45

Van Vugt, Victor 47, 57, 59
Van Zandt, Townes 60, 75, 76
Velvet Underground, the 5, 16, 33
Verlaine, Tom 5
Vickers, Robert 6, 24, 30, 95

Walkabouts, the 68
Walker, Clinton 7, 63
Wallace, Anne 115
Wallis, Mark 42, 92, 124

Waterboys, the 108
Waters, Roger 45
Watershed 32, 37, 91, 93
Watson, Jenny 115
Weir, Peter 66
Weiss, Ottocaro 113
what (artist) 114–15
White, Freddie 76
Whitely, Brett 32, 68
Whitlam, Gough 12–13
Willner, Hal 32
Willsteed, John 15, 23–4, 30–1
Withnail & I 69
Woolf, Virginia 86
Wydler, Thomas 46–8, 52–3

Yeats, W. B. 112